LIVING
TWO LIVES

MARRIED TO A MAN
& IN LOVE WITH A WOMAN

JOANNE FLEISHER

Lavender Visions Books: Philadelphia

LAVENDER Visions
Growing New Ways to See Your World

ISBN: 1461177464
ISBN-13: 9781461177463

With ongoing love & gratitude,
In memory of Judy

ACKNOWLEDGEMENTS

I am indebted to the women from my "Ask Joanne" Internet Message Board, who exposed their struggles and triumphs at a most critical time in their lives. They were my muse and inspiration for this book. My deepest thanks to August Tarrier, whose editing, encouragement and fresh perspective helped me complete the second edition of this book.

Many thanks to Maleka Fruean, who also offered her assistance, editing and marketing with a gracious willingness to work under time pressures.

I again want to thank my many friends and family members who willingly read chapters for the original book, offered feedback, and gave me lots of hope, including Marty Schlesinger, Polly O'Keefe, Frances Fisher, Cynthia Figueroa and my daughter, Lisa Vogel. My sister, Ellen Watson, my parents, Howard and Adele Fleisher, and my daughter, Beth Vogel, provided me with endless support when writing the first edition. My thanks to Kris Abney, Webmaster of the now-defunct Classic Dykes site, who invited me to monitor the "Ask Joanne" message board, which was originally a part of her website, and has been a constant support for many aspects of my work.

Lastly, there are no words that can adequately express my appreciation and love to my partner, Judy Mealing, who passed away prior to my writing the second edition of *Living Two Lives*. Throughout the writing of the first edition, she accepted my emotional vicissitudes, read every word that I wrote, and helped me edit, re-edit, think, and expostulate about the book from start to finish. Her encouragement and patience made this project possible.

TABLE OF CONTENTS

FOREWORD

"...the truth? You can't handle the truth."
— JACK NICHOLSON'S CHARACTER IN *A FEW GOOD MEN*

This may be the root of it all. We can't handle the truth. The truth interferes with our lives. It interferes in something as simple as not wanting to meet someone for dinner and not wanting to tell them why. The truth interferes with family relationships. We don't tell our father, our Aunt Tillie, or our children something that they might not understand or approve of. Our culture is set up not to rock the boat and to ostracize those who do. We are pack animals, and we have worked out an elaborate system of not telling the truth. We don't tell the truth even when someone is in danger with alcohol or domestic abuse. We don't confront them, or try to help their children, or help them, for that matter. Someone might get mad at us, we might be rejected, we might have to spend time doing something distasteful. We are used to living this way. Telling the truth to ourselves or someone else when it is frightening or unpopular makes us retreat, ignore it, hope it will go away. Everyone around us would rather us not deal with it as well. They don't want to look at their truths. We believe Jack Nicholson's words: we can't handle the truth.

If your truth is struggling with falling in love with a woman and you are currently married to a man, you have the right book in your hands. This book is thoughtfully composed. The author herself has gone through what you are going through, and she had children to worry about as well. She is a therapist and runs a website dedicated to these issues. She has thought this out and is careful to offer all her wisdom and experience, with no judgment and no formula for what you should do. Take it. You might think you can do this by yourself. But why? Take this book and the love and experience that is in it.

Living a lie, having an affair, being divorced, feeling selfish, questioning our mothering—I've just covered the worst nightmares of most women. This book addresses all of these and many more. Women aren't supposed to want for anything, we are supposed to give to everyone. You're changing your life either outside or inside or both forever, and it's all your own fault. Yipes! So much easier to blame our unhappiness on someone else. You could blame the woman you have fallen for, but honey, in the end it's still you who have hit this unexpected turn in the road and gone for it. Even if going for it is just in your mind.

The truth is that you deserve happiness. If you have children, they deserve to be taught what happiness is. You deserve love, respect, and caring. You deserve to treat others in your life with the same love and respect. This book offers ways of getting what you need and honoring those whose lives you are affecting. This book is filled with stories of women just like you who have struggled, and still struggle with what you are thigh deep in. Let yourself join a community of women who know what you are going through.

This journey is frightening because of how much you might have to give up. It's hard to face not just separation from your husband, but also the likely time you will spend apart from your children. You may also face being "divorced" by your family, friends, and neighbors who don't understand or don't know how to process the new information. You might end up with economic problems. You might face religious sanctions. This book is for you. It's full of ways to help you through the hard times and the times of ecstasy.

I myself have gone through transitions that others don't like, transitions that made me question my life more than I wanted to, transitions in which I lost many whom I loved. I couldn't stop being true to myself because of those losses. My son has gone through these changes with me, and he and I enjoy a respect and love that I am lucky to have. I have been able to create a loving adult relationship that is vibrant and alive and filled with honesty. I am not perfect, and I have made many mistakes, but without truth, I would be nothing.

I am also a counselor to women who have gone through many changes themselves, especially in the area of sexuality. I have counseled numerous women who are coming out, many of whom are coming out of heterosexual marriages and have fallen in love with women. It's a journey of great magnitude. You are embarking on a journey within yourself that will have you questioning everything. Just when you thought you were a grown up and that you had been through all the changes of life, bingo! Your life is in shambles. This inward journey will be worth it, however. No matter what you choose to do—come out, continue an affair or a series of affairs, create an open marriage, or stay in your marriage and forget women as lovers—none of these choices is perfect, none is without loss and gain. This life change is for love of yourself and your happiness. Look deep and long. You deserve it, and you and those around you will survive it. Perhaps you are ready for the truth, but even if you aren't, the truth is coming for you!

You are lucky to have this book. Joanne Fleisher has created something unique, filled with kindness, wisdom, practicality, honesty, and resourcefulness. This book is a testimony that many have gone before you and they have cleared the way. Your path to love is your own, and you deserve to travel it how you need to. Take this book along. Good luck on your path. May you meet many travelers who are ready for your truth.

JoAnn Loulan
Author, *Lesbian Sex* and other books

INTRODUCTION

Wisdom comes most easily to those who have the courage to embrace life without judgment and are willing to not know, sometimes for a long time.

— RACHEL NAOMI REMEN, M.D
KITCHEN TABLE WISDOM

If you are a married woman discovering your attraction to women, you are probably confused, upset, and excited all at the same time. You are not alone. I've traveled this path, and so have the many women who have contacted me through my therapy practice and the internet.

Many people believe that "coming out" is the process of disclosing your gay or lesbian sexual orientation to someone else—and it is that—but the most fundamental step in this process is coming out to *yourself*. Since the first edition of my book, I've worked with married women in therapy and spoken to hundreds of others through my online "Ask Joanne" Q & A message board. Most women who contact me don't know whether they are gay, bisexual, or just having an isolated experience. This book will help you understand the meaning of your attractions and how to proceed with your exploration. It will also provide important information to the people who

ʼou—spouses, female paramours, family members, and
.....ᵤ professionals.

I was in my early thirties, married with two young children, when
I fell in love with a woman. In 1978, people didn't have computers
with access to the internet and there were no organizations to offer
guidance. When I called the only resource in the phone book, a gay/
lesbian hotline, the responder was as clueless as I was. In tears, I
confessed that I was married and had fallen in love with a girlfriend.
The reply was, "So why are you crying?" I couldn't begin to explain
to this stranger the complications of falling in love with a woman
while being married. I then realized I had to go through my search
for understanding and direction alone. My ensuing experience of
dramatic upheaval became the basis for my commitment to helping
other women find their way.

When I began writing *Living Two Lives* in 2002, internet use had
opened the door to a different kind of access to resources for married
women who love women. Women could find information and support while maintaining privacy. In the nine years since writing the
first edition, I've seen another shift in our cultural climate. Coverage
of topics on gay issues is common in the entertainment, social, and
news media. Gay marriage is a hot topic being debated openly and
heatedly. While there is continued opposition from many parts of
the country, the fact that gay rights have become a political issue is
significant. Gay and lesbian characters appear regularly on TV series
and talk shows. Lesbian and gay culture, coming out stories, and
even alternative families with gay parents have reached Hollywood.
Actors, sports heroes, and politicians are coming out of hiding. Married women can now see their situation depicted and discussed in a
public forum. After I appeared in October 2006 on the Oprah Win-
frey show to discuss *Living Two Lives*, hundreds of married women

contacted me and joined my internet message board for married lesbians.

We've made inroads and there has been positive change, but homophobia is still entrenched in our religious and social institutions. If you're a married woman who has discovered an attraction to women, you may still feel isolated and alone. You may feel trapped in a lifestyle that doesn't reflect your internal reality and unable to reach out. You might have already begun to search for help privately.

If you picked up this book, it is very likely that you are ready to accept help. A shade may have lifted, you may feel alive for the first time, but reality demands that you confront some life-altering choices. As a married woman, you can expect criticism from other people because of society's general injunctions against homosexuality and infidelity. You may also face blame for breaking up the family. For all of us, cultural values can be deeply entrenched and unconsciously internalized, leading us to anticipate the worst possible scenarios. Fear is a huge barrier; without question, it takes enormous courage to confront your sexuality as an adult when so much is at stake: your marriage, your children, your entire way of life. It is my hope that this book will help you to realize that you do in fact have viable options.

In my therapy practice, I have worked with married women individually, in support groups, on the internet, and by telephone. I also moderate "Ask Joanne," an internet message board for married women who love women and are struggling with the related issues. Wives from all over the world contact me at my website, www.lavendervisions.com, and write to my advice column. Over the years, I have discovered that across geographical or cultural boundaries these women have one thing in common: they share a sense of isolation and confusion.

Throughout *Living Two Lives*, I provide vignettes from the message board and from clients to paint the rich and varied landscape of the married woman's journey. Although you may want more than anything for someone to simply tell you what to do, in fact you are the only one who can determine what is best for you. However, I've developed some guidelines to help you through this difficult time.

When I began my journey, I felt out of control. I had no idea what to expect or what was normal for a married woman in my situation. The purpose of this book is to help you identify the primary issues. Each chapter discusses different areas that require self-examination and growth as you work toward decision-making. When so much is changing in your world, it is difficult to know how to begin to sort things out. *Living Two Lives* provides a framework to explore your questions and make positive decisions. I've shared specific techniques for managing the erratic emotions so common in this transition. Many of the coping strategies introduced in this book will also apply to the other people in your life, as each person involved is undergoing a difficult struggle.

When there are children involved, you may spend a lot of time worrying about how your decisions will affect them. They didn't ask for this, you may think. They will need to adjust to your changing sexual identity and possibly your family structure. As you become more resilient, you will be better prepared to help your kids. I have offered some guidelines for helping them at different stages of development. My two daughters had some areas of adjustment, which I will share, yet they were grateful to grow up feeling loved by many. I learned that their successes and their difficulties were rarely related to my sexuality.

This book is designed to help you begin to expand your vision and range of possibilities, and to support you in suspending your judgments about the variety of ways women have chosen to live their lives. You too can make changes, be sensitive to the needs of your loved ones, live a life that is more fulfilling, and be proud of who you are.

Decision-making usually involves trial and error, and when we do come to a decision, it is rarely final or irreversible. As a married woman discovering her attraction to a woman, I often ended up making choices just to end my interminable fence-sitting. I kept changing directions, and I was terribly frustrated that I couldn't seem to come to the one decision that was the right one. But each time I changed my mind, I learned something important. Try to show yourself the same compassion as you would your family members or close friends. The issues here are deeply ethical and require self-examination. When I betrayed my marriage vows, my husband was surprised and hurt, and I will always feel some sadness for the pain I caused him. But with time I have learned how critical it was for me to be able to forgive myself for what I didn't know or understand prior to marriage. This is an extremely opportune moment to examine your belief systems with a critical eye in order to determine which ones make sense to you now. This process nearly always takes longer than you wish and requires tremendous patience.

In this second edition, not only have I updated information, but I've also added a final chapter, "Ask Joanne: Questions from Readers." This chapter provides excerpts from the ongoing conversation I've been having with many of my readers over the past nine years since the first edition was written. It addresses fears women have concerning husbands' reactions, coming out without a partner, and myths about lesbian relationships. Are lesbian relationships unstable or short-lived? Do lesbians hook up and commit too quickly?

These are complex questions and they deserve thoughtful and compassionate responses. In my own journey, I have discovered the gains and losses in every decision, and realized that to truly appreciate the gains, you must address the losses. The more losses facing you, the more difficult your decision will be. Recently, my partner of thirty years passed away. From this painful loss I developed additional coping skills to manage my grief. I learned the importance of silence to help me access my feelings. I had always avoided solitude, but in this instance it became my ally as I had to face the challenge of letting go of old beliefs and unmet dreams and opening to new ideas and inevitable changes. Such lessons will help you, too. Like me, you will need to grieve and to let go in order to move forward.

It is *how* you view your life changes that can make all the difference. Facing your uncertainty with confidence and trusting your feelings while identifying and questioning your beliefs is the foundation for wise choices. When you eventually come to your resolution, you'll be able to honor the role of the painful times in helping you to find abiding joy. Whether you decide to leave your marriage or to stay, you are beginning a new life chapter. It is my great hope that this book will meet you where you are in your current transition and help you face any of life's upheavals with resiliency and resolve.

CHAPTER 1

THE QUESTIONING BEGINS

I am married and have been in a relationship with a lesbian woman for the past year. I'm confused about my sexual orientation. I adore my girlfriend and can't imagine life without her. With three small children, I feel so selfish when I consider breaking up my family. I'm not sure I could live with myself shaking up their world.

— FLO

When a married woman suddenly feels an attraction to another woman, the experience often turns her world upside down. She is filled with questions and uncertainty. One client described herself as always "surrounded by a fog." Her foundation had been rocked by her discovery. She no longer trusted many of the beliefs she had about herself, her marriage, or her values.

If this is the first time you have fallen in love with a woman, at first you probably won't see yourself differently—this is something that just happened. But it won't be long before you begin to feel a sense of alienation. You may wonder, *Am I supposed to see myself differently? How will other people view me? If other people start to see me* differently, am I different? How will this affect my marriage, my children, my family?

On the other hand, it may not be the first time you have felt attracted to a woman. If you denied earlier attractions by tucking your feelings away, you may need to revisit the questions you have avoided. Whether these feelings are new or re-emerging you might wonder, Why is this happening now?

The answer is unclear; the human psyche is a mystery. There are certain moments in life when dormant issues emerge to consciousness, when events can cause you to examine your assumptions about who you are. Perhaps you have reached a time of more maturity and you have more resources, internally and externally, to handle questions about your sexuality.

You are starting a journey of self-examination, a reconstruction of your core identity. There is renewed attention to essential questions of being: Who am I? What is love? What is meaningful? How do I create that meaning for myself? Most women seem to need a minimal of two years and up to six years or more to reach a comfortable understanding and acceptance of their newly discovered sexual identity. The beginning of this passage is not the time to make any major decisions.

> The advice of many is to take your time, but timing is an individual thing. My seven-month transition seemed like seven years or seven days, depending. You are entitled to be happy. And yes, you will be sad along the way. It's part of the journey. In the end, to BE me is worth it. I still have a long way to go, but I'm finally headed in the right direction.
>
> — ROBERTA

You can start to create some order by defining the questions you need to answer.

At the start, there are two primary concerns: how will this attraction affect my marriage and family, and how will it impact me as a person and my sexual identity? These two issues become intertwined, each affecting the other. At this stage, the challenge is to *tolerate the ambiguity* of not yet having the answers, perhaps the most difficult aspect of the process.

The confluence of these two issues are reflected in the following messages:

I am more turned on by women than I am by men. I've been married for twenty-five years and have never been satisfied. Am I just unhappy in this marriage, or am I really a lesbian?

— JOYCE

I'm forty years old and on my third unsuccessful marriage. The only time I really feel happy is when I'm around women who are gay, but due to the strict way I was raised, this lifestyle has never been an option. How can I accept this way of life?

— SUE

I am married, and for the last three years, I've been involved with a woman. This is new to both of us. We have found great joy in each other, but neither of us feels any attraction to other women. I don't know if I am really gay, and I have trouble accepting the label. Is a person gay/lesbian if that attraction is felt only for one person?

— ALICE

In order to identify your questions, it will help to separate the two categories. For example, you might ask yourself early on, *Do I want to save my marriage?* You may also be asking, *Am I a lesbian?* Each will have an impact on the other, depending on your answers. For example, Nancy asks, "Is it really possible to be married, have sex with a man, and still be a lesbian?"

If you know with certainty that you don't want to risk your marriage, you may decide to work on the marriage first and avoid going further into your sexuality questions. On the other hand, you may feel that delving into your sexual orientation is not a choice.

> *I was told by my husband, "If you are going to be a lesbian, you are not going to be part of this family." IF I was GOING TO BE?. . . when will people ever understand this is not a choice . . . it's acknowledgment (for me anyway). I may choose to ACT on it, but choose to be? No.*
>
> — ANNA

Anna is clear that her sexual orientation is lesbian. Her choices concern how to incorporate her sexuality into her life. Women who are less certain about their sexual orientation will need to pay more attention to identity issues. Kate says, "Once you let the genie out of the bottle, she's not going back in." If you feel this way, you know your primary focus is to understand your sexual transformation.

Issues Related to Marriage

- *Am I dissatisfied with my marriage?*
- *Do I want to work on my marriage?*
- *Should I tell my husband? If so, how?*
- *Do I want a divorce?*

- *If I don't want divorce, what are my options?*
- *How will my discovery affect my husband and children?*

If you are not sure of your sexual identity, you may want to work toward increasing communication and intimacy within the marriage. Since you are already in this relationship, you will have to deal with it no matter where your exploration takes you. When there are problems, they often relate to a lack of intimacy, a power imbalance, and/ or sexual problems. It helps to know what is or is not working in your marriage and why, in order to make good decisions for you and your family. In my own therapy, I began to explore the reasons behind my affair. I had married my high school boyfriend a year after my college graduation. We had a long history together and were happy for much of the marriage. Even though my husband and I had some problems, I thought our relationship was just fine until I looked more closely. What I wanted in a mate at age twenty-two was different than what I desired in my early thirties. I was longing for more intimacy from my husband and often felt lonely. Like me, many women have a sense that their husband is a good man and their marriage is satisfying. Yet there may be something they haven't acknowledged about what caused them to look elsewhere for their intimacy.

Despite marital problems, if you have a strong *desire* to hold onto your marriage, and your husband feels the same, it may be possible to make the relationship work. There are strong qualifiers: both spouses must have the will to work things out. Chapter 8, "Your Options" shares various creative solutions that women have found to maintain their marriages.

Issues Related to Sexual Identity

- *Is this about one woman or women in general?*

- *Am I lesbian, bisexual, or heterosexual?*
- *When did this begin?*
- *Why is this happening now?*
- *What are my fears about being gay?*
- *How do I deal with homophobia—mine, my husband's, my children's, my family's, society's?*

When women first fall in love or feel a powerful attraction to a woman, they may not jump to the conclusion that they are lesbian. It takes time and experience to learn how extensive the attractions are. Married women often are thrown into crisis when they begin to consider the possibility of being gay. Homophobia, both internalized and societal, is a huge factor in the struggle for many women, and the logistics of exploring your sexuality are difficult within the context of marriage.

Situations That Lead to Questioning

Marital Unhappiness

Unhappiness in your marriage may lead you to reevaluate what relationships bring you satisfaction or even joy. My marital difficulties were ongoing for a few years before I first began to feel attracted to other women. The problems were not exceptional as marital issues go, but the dissatisfaction prompted my search for what was missing. Sometimes when women feel restless or tired of the routine of married life, they become vulnerable to having affairs. Loneliness or lack of intimacy in the marriage are common

complaints from women who begin to explore romantic relationships with women.

Life Transitions

*It all started about two years ago after I lost my father. His death
made me reevaluate my life, and my true sentiments came out!!
My feelings seem to be getting stronger and stronger, and I just
don't know what to do about it.*

— SYLVIE

*I began questioning my sexuality as I was going through an
early menopause; I'm fifty. I found myself, for the first time in my
life, desiring sexual intimacy. I mean not only with my husband,
but (surprise!) with women. I was so frightened to admit this to
my husband, to my children, and mostly to myself!*

— CALLIE

*Being thirty-nine, I hit that midlife crisis point in my life. I started
really looking at the life I have been living. I asked myself some
hard questions . . . Who am I? What do I want out of life? What
makes me happy? What have I always wanted to do with my
life and why haven't I done it?*

—RANDA

Buying a house, graduating from school, discovering you are
pregnant or infertile, and having your children leave home are the
types of life junctures that require contemplation. Any transition
can initiate the assessment of your life choices, even entering a new
decade in life.

A Passionate Attraction or Longing

Once I experienced love from a woman, there was no going back. Lovemaking with my husband was nice. He is a very good lover and gentle man, but making love with a woman made all the songs and fireworks come alive for me.

— MARJORIE

Since I've been married, I have had several very intense crushes on women who are pretty butch in their dress and manner. Lately, it has just overwhelmed me, and I feel that I must make a lifestyle change.

— LOIS

When this new attraction arises for the first time, it hits like a bolt of lightning. It seems to make little difference whether your first female love becomes an intimate friendship, an affair, or an unrequited love. The experience is unsettling. The depth of the connection may feel like an entirely new experience. This epiphany usually causes women to look back over their prior intimacies and to reexamine them within the context of this new powerful attraction.

One woman told me that she fell into a severe depression when she retired. She began to feel a familiar, desperate longing that never was satisfied by the relationship with her husband. The pressures of work no longer distracted her from old feelings that she had known, but avoided, all her life.

It seems we married gals either first have an incredibly passionate affair with a woman whom we fall deeply, wildly in love with before making life changes, or we experience this incredible longing, which also feels like a wild, first time love, for a woman we barely know, but for whom we have this strange, overwhelming passion. I understand the affairs, but don't understand the distant longings.

— SHARONA

The mysteries of love are difficult to explain. Falling in love usually includes a projection of our beliefs about who the other person seems to be, physical attraction, and a development of emotional intimacy with someone. Women begin to realize their attractions to other women in many different ways: reacting to a woman's email messages (which can prove to be quite different than the way she acts in person); falling in love with a teacher, therapist, or a yoga instructor (where image plays a large part); feeling excited by sexual encounters between two women in the media; or developing a crush on a friend or a coworker. Some women fall in love when they become very close to another woman; some fall in love when they watch a woman from a distance. Imagination plays a part in all forms of love. Longing is a powerful feeling. The challenge is to turn the energy of our internal longings into action. It may seem safer to keep this feeling inside you than to do the necessary work to become available for a full relationship or to find a woman who is equally ready to be involved. If you are longing for the love of a woman, you might not yet be prepared to do anything more than begin to recognize the feelings.

Unrequited Love

I am in my early fifties, married with adult children, and was bowled over about a year ago when, out of the blue, I fell heavily for another woman. There is no hope of a relationship, because she is in a great lesbian relationship. But I cannot forget her, no matter how hard I try.

— LUCY

Grief over the realization that a relationship will never develop is often more difficult than mourning a relationship that is ending. If you are experiencing unrequited love, you face not only the unsettling question of sexual orientation but also the pain of never knowing what the relationship could have been. You are struggling to let go of your fantasy.

Whether your lover is the object of an unattainable dream or she leaves you after an affair, you may be shocked at the level of grief involved in your recovery process. It may be the first time you have fallen in love. In my case, I fell hard, but my girlfriend decided that I was a poor prospect for the potential long-term relationship she desired. I was years behind her in the process of defining my sexuality, and I was still married. She left town to follow a more promising partner.

I felt utterly abandoned, knowing I was facing huge decisions alone. I fell into a deep depression for about three months as I dealt with the loss of my lover. I worried that I might never again have the level of closeness and intimacy that I had felt for the first time. Pain and fear are hallmarks of this initial exploration. Sometimes they overshadow the excitement and romantic feelings that also herald a new chapter of life.

Therapy Stimulates Questions

When a client begins to work in therapy, it is not uncommon to discover aspects of the self that were previously unconscious. Many women suppress memories associated with early fears of facing lesbian tendencies. Therefore, married women sometimes become aware of same-sex attractions in the course of therapy. It's not unusual for women to fall in love with other women while in therapy—and at times with their therapist.

I'm forty-five and just finding out through therapy and my own honesty with myself that I have had attractions toward women since I was young.

— CARLA

During the past year, I have been in therapy to come to terms with my childhood trauma. In addition, I've begun to question my sexual identity. I care for my spouse very deeply, but I have no real desire or sexual attraction for him. Recently I've become extremely attracted to a female coworker. I am also discovering I'm in love with my female therapist.

— DARLENE

Both women may be reaching a new awareness of unconscious attractions. Darlene's description suggests she is having "transference" in her therapy. Transference love is based on an idealized view of the therapist, who appears wise, nonjudgmental, and all accepting. Secrets and intimacies are shared in therapy, but they are one-sided. These circumstances can create an opportunity for imagining the therapist to be just what the patient needs her to be. Outside of the therapy room, in other parts of life, a love relationship with a peer makes many more demands of the individual—demands for emotional, empathetic, and sexual reciprocity. It is important to differentiate whether this feeling of love is a fantasy about your therapist or a sexual orientation issue, or possibly both. Usually, it is best to try to work this question out directly with the therapist, even if it feels uncomfortable.

Values Conflicts

Experiences that lead you to question your sexual orientation may also challenge your personal values and priorities. Tremendous dissonance occurs when questions arise such as:

- *Can I continue to build my life around a religious community that would reject me if they knew of my same-sex attractions?*
- *Can I pursue a more authentic life if I believe divorce is irreparably harmful to children?*
- *Can I be a devoted mom if I leave my husband or become a part-time mother?*
- *Can I respect myself if I am gay?*
- *Can I tolerate other people's negative judgment of me?*

Homophobia

When women first come to a clear self-acknowledgment of their sexual identity, it often throws them into crisis. And why wouldn't it? You may suddenly realize that your life experiences don't match your desires and fantasies. If you avoided early same-sex attractions, there may be some deep fears residing inside you about identifying as homosexual. Your feelings and beliefs about being gay may require exploration.

Sometimes I wish I could go back and be in denial again. What a dichotomy, to finally feel whole and understand the reason behind much pain and frustration throughout my life, and at the same time feel terror at the mere thought of coming out.

—LORI

For some women homophobia was so powerful in their adolescent years that they consciously ignored their natural feelings in favor of finding a man to marry. You may have developed a mask for the world that eventually made it difficult for even you to identify what was authentic. Audrey's beliefs about lesbians made her feel that she could never fit into gay culture or find a lesbian who would be attractive to her.

I always sort of knew I was lesbian, but when I was a teenager, I was so naïve. I thought homosexuality was very rare and I thought lesbians were all very butch, fat, unattractive women. I believed what friends always told me, that women became lesbian because they were too ugly to get a man. I really knew nothing at all about gay people except all the homophobic stereotypes that I was taught. It was profoundly depressing to me to think that I loved women but the women I wanted were all straight and would never love me.

— AUDREY

A powerful way to combat internalized homophobia—those strong feelings of fear or discomfort about being gay—is to be in the company of lesbians, both married and single. It can be challenging to break through the stereotypes about who lesbians are and what defines the lesbian lifestyle.

In my Gay After Marriage Workshops, married women travel great distances to find support and information. Often, at the end of the first session, women remark with astonishment, "We all appear to be normal." Many express surprise that the group has so many attractive women. In this way, group members confront their prejudices and myths about lesbians.

Not everyone has the opportunity to participate in a married women's support group, but there are other ways to challenge preconceived ideas. Throughout my journey of discovery, I tried to talk to as many women as I could who identified themselves as lesbian or bisexual. Some women go to bookstores or libraries to find lesbian literature. Today women have the internet where they can communicate with others or read messages from women like themselves. Information and direct contact all help in your process of defeating internalized homophobia.

Internalized homophobia can undermine your ability to build a committed relationship with a woman. Keeping your life secret, feeling ashamed of your most intimate relationship, and isolating from friends usually lead to general anxiety and unhappiness. It's helpful to confront your fears and biases now, before you make important decisions about your future. Liza's story, in the following message, exemplifies the way internalized homophobia creates enormous stress in even a most loving relationship.

I thought of myself as a strong, confident woman all my life. Even thought so as I met a woman, fell in love, left a marriage, bought my own home, and started a new life. My children are doing great. I, however, am running as fast as I can now from the "lesbian" label. I have broken up with my girlfriend. Thinking of choosing the straight life because of my fear of being "discovered" by my work acquaintances, any professional people, or parents of my children's friends. My girlfriend is devastated. Fear is right on the money when describing my mindset. After hurrying through the first two years of this journey, I think I'll sit for a while and ponder what in the hell I am doing and where I am going.

— LIZA

Traditional Family Values

Just because you are attracted to a woman doesn't mean that you hold a particular set of values. You may live in and share the same values of a community that has little tolerance for difference. Polly came to a support group at the age of fifty-one. She saw herself as an upstanding citizen, an accountant with Republican Party values. Her husband was the minister of a conservative Presbyterian church. Polly was a supportive wife, sacrificing when necessary for the good of her husband's career. She always expected life would be good for their four kids.

My kids have a wonderful life. They live in a big house with a beautiful yard, attend an excellent school, and have lots of friends. We are the perfect "leave-it to-Beaver" family. I still want that way of life. It's hard to even imagine leaving my husband, not knowing if I can find such comfort and stability with a woman.

— POLLY

Polly's love affair with a female coworker conflicted with many of her values in her seemingly predictable world. Divorce was not a part of her plan, and it would be detrimental to her husband's job. The idea of a lesbian life didn't look very hopeful or appealing to her. She had raised her children in a traditional nuclear family, and she was afraid that any deviation would harm her kids. Everyone in their community looked at her family as the ideal. In fact, she herself always believed that image, and she was invested in holding onto it. The life changes Polly anticipated so conflicted with her values that her journey was especially long and uneven.

Feelings of Obligation

How can I leave a man who is very ill? How can I abandon a person who has no one else but me? How do I stay in a life that is not mine because I can't handle the guilt?

— FLORENCE

Having a husband who is ill or a child with a disability adds further heartache to the situation. When Florence contacted me, she was looking for a way to continue living with her husband, while knowing that she wanted to be with a woman. She was married to a man with a degenerative disease that left him dependent on her for his daily survival. Florence had been aware of her attraction to women for seven years.

She felt guilty about wanting to leave her husband and confused about how to create a fulfilling life for herself. She was caught between her desire to follow through on her marital, even humane, commitment, and her need to live as a lesbian. If you face a similar value conflict, you must take your time and recognize that there can be no easy solution. You are the best judge of what you must sacrifice for your peace of mind.

If Your Husband "Saved You"

Marriage, for some women, is the first experience of a stable relationship. Women who have chaotic, dysfunctional family backgrounds often marry to escape those destructive relationships. Sometimes husbands provide a steadiness that brings comfort and security to their lives. Hurting your husband is difficult for any woman, but hurting your rescuer feels like a deeper level of betrayal. It might take you longer to accept your sexuality than other women.

This is a good time to reexamine the unresolved family issues to keep yourself moving toward your goals.

Your Comfortable Lifestyle

Because of the gender inequities in our culture, most women experience a decline in their standard of living when they get divorced. A life of material ease is important to many women. You face additional stress if you have not worked outside the home. If you divorce, you may need to find a job to support yourself. The choice between a dissatisfying but economically expedient life and a life of loving fulfillment with financial struggle is a difficult dilemma.

In recent years, I've noticed a sign of some cultural changes favoring women. On occasion, I meet women who have been supporting their husbands financially and depending on them for home and childcare. If you are the primary economic support for the family, you may worry about your husband's ability to become self-sufficient. You will need to take into account your additional financial burden if you decide to leave him.

Religious Conflict

I come from a Christian fundamentalist family. I feel such shame, and I think it stems from being taught and believing that homosexuality is abnormal.

— KATHERINE

I was straight my entire life until, at age forty-two, I found myself with an enormous crush on a woman. After that crush, I continued to find myself attracted to women only and ended up having a brief affair with one. I have been unable to get myself to pray to love my husband more because of how right being with a woman feels.

— ELIZABETH

A woman who feels a strong spiritual connection with the religion of her childhood may experience anguish when that religion is unwelcoming or downright hostile to lesbians or bisexuals. If you have found community support in a church that fosters homophobia, you are likely to internalize fear, hatred, or even disgust toward homosexuality. One woman wrote that she dated women when she was in her twenties but didn't want to hurt her parents. When she became involved in her church, she started to believe her attractions were influenced by Satan. She tried to pray her feelings away, tried to ignore them, or detached herself from her sexual feelings. Eventually she married to avoid facing her homosexuality.

Sometimes a member of the clergy or someone from your religious community who understands the tenets of your faith can help you to sort out the moral conflicts. In some churches, it is hard to find support, but, increasingly, there are individuals and communities within all the dominant religious institutions in our country that accept gays and lesbians. In addition, specific groups representing the religious traditions are run by and directed to gay, lesbian, and bisexual people.

Some women don't feel a personal conflict but are confronted by the religious beliefs of their family. If your family's religious beliefs oppose homosexuality, you can anticipate their concerns. Your parents may reject you or develop fears that you will be rejected by God or by their church community. They may believe you are headed for hell. As you become more certain of the decisions you are making for the sake of your personal integrity, you will be better prepared to talk to family members. There's no need to rush into conversation. Wait until you are more confident about your decisions.

Separating the Issues

Until I went through menopause, I just thought I didn't have a sex drive. But then my emotions for women began to emerge, and our marital sex life dwindled. I began to question my sexual identity for the first time.

— MARIAN

My husband and I always found reasons for my lack of desire. The big one was that I was drugged and raped for hours by two guys before I met my husband. The other reason was that I grew up in a VERY sheltered, Bible-reading, conservative home.

— MERRY

Most women tend to connect a myriad of issues with their sexuality: hormonal changes (premenstrual or menopausal), child abuse, sexual abuse, unhappy marriages, mental illness (mood disorders or post-traumatic stress disorder, dysfunctional families), and so on. If you are making this kind of association, you are, in essence, searching for the pathology behind your desire. The American Psychological Association and the American Psychiatric Association do not consider homosexuality a dysfunction or pathological.

From the ages of eight to eleven, I was molested by a lesbian teenager. I never told anyone because she threatened to hurt me if I did. During that period, I began to masturbate and fantasize about her. She became my secret lesbian lover. I am now forty years old and married with children. I still fantasize about being with a woman. Looking back over my life, I can truly say I have been a lesbian in spirit since I was a teenager but never acted out my fantasies. Today, I feel the desire to satisfy my curiosity is stronger than ever. But I am afraid of the loss and hurt, and the pain I may cause my children, for satisfying my own secret desires.

— MONA

This kind of experience can cause confusion later in life, especially for women who are questioning their sexual orientation. It is important that you distinguish between abuse and sexual preference. As I told Mona, therapy can help you to better understand how that early experience has affected your current relationships, trust, and self-image. An early sexual experience may have awakened your response to women. However, if you find yourself blaming your same-sex attractions on the abuse, keep in mind that most abuse survivors are heterosexual. Therapy is a good place to start to work on healing your negative associations of abuse with homosexuality.

Mona has had these longings for many years, and her message suggests that she is lesbian, but she has to reach her own definition. It is nearly impossible for any woman to explore either sexual abuse or sexual orientation without creating upheaval in her marriage. If you have experienced abuse similar to Mona's, give yourself plenty of time to explore the myriad issues involved. Some women wonder if they heal from the abuse, whether they will stop feeling attracted to other women. This would be unusual, because sexual orientation is not something that can or should be healed; it is a natural preference.

If the perpetrator of your sexual abuse was male, you still might question whether your same-sex attraction is just a reaction to the abuse. The same principles apply. Separate the abuse from your sexual orientation. When you are able to view either straight or gay sex as a potentially healthy, loving experience, then you can eventually find your way to your true sexual identity.

I just noticed that talking with men makes me extremely uncomfortable. I feel really unsettled with myself, and I immediately think that they don't take me seriously and just think "SEX." I am so much more comfortable talking with women and have always been... I am wondering if this is all coming from having been sexually abused as a child by a man, or if this has more to do with my attraction in general to women.

— TERRY

The self-exploration necessitated by a sexual "reorientation" often reveals new information. It is hard to ever know the direct cause of specific feelings that people have. A history of sexual abuse often causes a survivor to feel uncomfortable with people who remind her of the perpetrator. On the other hand, many women feel less comfortable with men than with women. Women often say that the feeling of "coming home" that occurs when becoming close to a woman is due partially to the level of comfort they feel. They can be themselves. I felt relief with the absence of gender role expectations when I became intimate with a woman. I also discovered I was more able to experience and express my personal power with a woman than I was with men. Early experiences, removal of gender expectations, and sexual orientation may all have an impact on your comfort level with men.

Your search for possible causes of your same-sex attractions should be examined with dispassion. Even if another issue is connected to your sexuality, it shouldn't invalidate your attractions or suggest that homosexuality must be viewed as a dysfunction. If you question your sexual identity because of difficult life events, it may help to separate these issues with a gay-friendly therapist. It is critical to reach an acceptance of your sexuality as a positive aspect of yourself.

Taking It Slowly

This period of initial exploration can be incredibly frustrating. You are working on life-altering questions and deserve all the time that it takes to establish your questions and become comfortable with your answers. Women often wish for shortcuts to solutions and, thus, make impulsive decisions. Others drag out decision-making. Either approach may be an avoidance of pain or of taking responsibility for making the decisions. If you are fully conscious, there is no way around the pain. However, this is an opportunity for you to grow in self-understanding and integrity. As much as you may want to know the end of your story, you will benefit most by patiently waiting for it to unfold. Marta, who has survived a rough journey, offers these words of solace:

> *I know myself better and feel more alive than I ever have. To know sorrow is to make the joy all that more precious. There is no right answer for everyone, just an attempt at living life honestly, completely, and joyfully.*
>
> — MARTA

WHAT YOU CAN DO NOW

Remind yourself: Be patient, and honor the importance of doing all that is necessary to make these important decisions.

Ask yourself this question: What caused you to begin to question your sexuality and/or your marriage?

Practice this technique for handling anxiety: Use a calming breathing exercise. Deep breathing has a physiological basis for calming the body. When we are anxious, our breathing becomes quicker and more shallow. The goal is to consciously slow down and deepen the quality of your breathing. Practice this brief breathing exercise five to ten times a day:

- *Take a slow, deep breath, in through your nose.*
- *Hold your breath for a count of two.*
- *Then release your breath through your lips, feeling the muscles in your chest, shoulders, neck, and stomach relax, allowing the tension to flow out.*
- *Repeat this for thirty seconds.*

Take one step: Begin keeping a journal, even if you only jot down a paragraph or two each day.

Keeping a record of your innermost thoughts and feelings is an excellent way of learning about yourself. Over time, it will also help you identify ways that you have grown and changed. Use the journal, also, to answer the questions posed at the end of each chapter.

CHAPTER 2

DISCOVERING YOUR SEXUAL IDENTITY

I always thought you just would know these kinds of things when you are younger, not in your mid-thirties. Although I was curious as a teen, I thought they were normal thoughts people had. How do I now make such a life-altering decision without feeling guilt?

— JANET

It takes courage and ingenuity to explore your sexual identity as an adult. Women often feel both confused and ashamed when they begin to question their heterosexuality after marriage. They might wonder how and why these new feelings are happening so late in life. Many of us were taught that our sexual identity is formed during adolescence—the "proper" time for burgeoning sexual interest and experimentation. This clearly wasn't my experience. I was influenced by both my parents' expectations and by my unquestioning acceptance of what my peers were doing. In my sheltered upbringing during the late 1950s, I didn't even know that girls could be lesbian. Admittedly, times have changed. There is far more information available today, but, like me, you may not have recognized evidence of lesbian sexuality during your adolescence. Our early process of exploration is inevitably influenced by our culture, which is rife with negativity toward homosexuality. Even with increased societal openness, many adolescents who feel they are different are fearful of sharing their thoughts or concerns with their friends.

As we develop and individuate, we learn more about ourselves and our sexuality. As we mature and begin to question ourselves and others, we are in a much better position to understand our sexual identity. Like many preteens, I didn't think much about the issue of sexuality. I followed my peer group norms: I talked about boys, acted interested, and wanted to be popular. In my teens, I mostly responded to the boys who were interested in me. Once my hormones became active, I had my share of relationships with guys. But I couldn't understand why I didn't feel as "in love" as many of my friends did. Secretly, I thought there was something wrong with me. The need for acceptance is so powerful during this period that it explains why many adolescents do not pursue desires that would lead them to be ostracized from the group. Our culture teaches girls to be relational by focusing their attention on others, and yet if we are to learn about ourselves we need to focus inward, which often feels selfish. Many women don't learn to pay attention to their own needs and desires until they are more mature. I didn't start questioning my sexual satisfaction until my mid to late twenties, when my friends began to talk about sex. At that time, I began to wonder if my sexual and relational life could be better.

Every person is entitled to explore and express her authentic sexuality without the burden of shame. Acknowledging and understanding your sexual identity is fundamental to the development of a healthy ego. If your adolescent attractions were focused on girls, you may have ignored them or felt pressure to change. When grown women have their first romantic attachment to a woman, they often speak of feeling like a teenager again. In fact, as you examine your sexual identity, you may move through many of the steps that adolescents take when exploring their sexuality. Some of those include sexual experimentation and risky behavior. I can hardly believe some of the places I made out with my girlfriend at the age of thirty-two and the ways I risked being caught. It can feel embarrassingly adolescent when you need to learn about the cues of flirtation or interest between women, when you find yourself becoming obsessively involved with romance, or when you end up feeling emotionally volatile (which no longer can be blamed on raging hormones!).

I've come to the realization that I'm finally experiencing my awkward adolescence, something I somehow muted when I was actually going through puberty. I'm discovering the moodiness: "no one likes/understands me," "who cares?" insecurity, etc., Feelings that I don't recall having too much when I was younger and that I certainly haven't felt a whole heck of a lot of as an adult. Let me tell you, it's a tad embarrassing at times.

— RHONA

You may not be even as lucky as Rhona. Many women have gone through a difficult adolescence only to be experiencing it again, later in life. The good news is that this upheaval usually subsides once you have adjusted to the changes of your transition. Even better, you may find yourself feeling, for the first time in your life, that you can love and be loved from the core of your being.

The difficulty of redefining your sexuality when you're an adult is not just about the stigma of being lesbian or bisexual, but is more likely tied up with confusion regarding the changing nature of your sexual attractions. It can be as puzzling to you as it is to the people around you. You may not feel secure about making any decision without having some understanding of how your current situation "happened" to you. Until recently, the dominant societal belief was that all people are rigidly defined as either heterosexual, homosexual, bisexual, or asexual, but the current discourse about human sexuality isn't nearly so black and white. Today, many young women who are attracted to women don't identify with any of the above labels. If they've had attractions or relationships with other women, they often label themselves "queer." This term has become a catch-all category that includes all sexual minorities who are not heterosexual or living within gender norms. However, some people find the label "queer" offensive because it has been used in derisive ways and is viewed by some as a politically radical term.

If you are confused about how to define yourself, it's understandable. Current research is changing the notion that we have a static sexual orientation, especially for women. Sexual attractions, behavior, and identity are fluid throughout life. When you look back over your sexual history, you may find that it is more variable than you might have initially believed. I experienced attractions to women for the first time in my late twenties, but many women recall attractions and experimentation with females much earlier than that. Studies from the 1950s and 1960s revealed that people's sexual habits were often fluid, but the concept of sexual fluidity was never emphasized. In 1979, researchers William H. Masters and Virginia E. Johnson found in a study of lesbians that 32 percent of their sample had been married previously. In his 1978 study, Fritz Klein found that 42 percent of a gay and lesbian sample had been married, with equal distribution between the men and women. A 1992 study of three hundred lesbians by Paula C. Rust of Hamilton College in New York supported other research by the National Institute of Health that most women who identify as lesbian are not 100 percent drawn to other women. Rather, they are inclined to say they *prefer* women over men. Some have relations with men after coming out as lesbians.

Most lesbian women I meet look like, and sometimes act like, men. This mannish aspect of gay women is a turn-off for me. Sometimes I feel too feminine to be a lesbian.
P.S. I don't even have short hair!

— FREIDA

You might assume that if you are lesbian, you are a particular kind of person, an idea that is promulgated by societal beliefs. Today, though, there are fewer pressures to assume one sexual identity. Trying to fit strictly into any category denies you access to the many dimensions of human sexuality and human experience. When I first came out, I thought I would have to leave behind my more feminine garb. I still like to get dressed up for special occasions, so I do. Many of the women who attend the married women's support groups worry about their desire to wear makeup or whether they will find other feminine women who identify as lesbian. These fears are based on lingering stereotypes of lesbians. You may be misled in assuming you can identify a lesbian by her appearance. Some women feel most comfortable without makeup or dresses. Historically, these non-conformist women found a freedom in the lesbian community that is not as acceptable in mainstream society. While life can be more difficult for women who don't fit gender stereotypes, there is more acceptance in the lesbian community of such differences. However, as lesbian culture becomes more in vogue, the lesbian norm often mirrors the mainstream appearance of femininity. My best advice is to continue to be yourself as you explore your sexual identity. At this time, your greatest challenge may be to accept the fluidity and multifaceted quality of your sexuality.

*I am married and involved with a woman who proudly iden-
tifies as a lesbian. First, I labeled myself as gay, because that
seemed to be the only reasonable explanation for my behavior. Now? I identify, if I must, as bisexual. I am not an "on-the-
fence" lesbian. I am truly attracted to both sexes. I find it hard to
see that in the gay community there is such prejudice against
bisexuality.*

— SALINA

Society's notions shape and limit our own sexual definition. People often feel anxious when a woman doesn't accept easy labels like
"gay" or "straight" to define her sexual experiences or attractions.
Because clear labels are easier to understand, you may feel pressured to find a label that fits you. When I first revealed my affair with
a woman to a group of close liberal-minded friends, they seemed
excited about my "change" of sexual orientation. In their eyes, I
had taken on an admirable aura of difference. Their response upset
and confused me. I felt no different inside—I had merely become
sexually involved with my friend. I believed that I was still a suburban housewife and mother doing the same mundane chores and
involved in the same interesting activities as always. I didn't want
respect or rejection because of this action I had taken. I didn't feel
different, but I was experiencing difference through other people's
eyes. While one part of me was changing, the rest was still the same.

The pressure to determine the right label for yourself may also
be connected to your decision-making process. Many of the married
women whom I counsel believe that if they knew for certain they
were lesbian, it would resolve the question of whether they should
stay married. It can be disheartening to realize that one's sexuality
is not always so clear, nor is the decision to leave the marriage, even
when you feel certain that you are lesbian.

We all have a variety of identities that define us. When we focus exclusively on one aspect of our self-definition, we may lose sight of the many other facets of our being. Labeling one aspect of ourselves does not necessarily determine our life choices, which means that the search for identity is often defined by ambiguity instead of certainty. In *Lesbian and Bisexual Identities*, Audre Lorde wrote about this idea: "As a black lesbian feminist comfortable with the many different ingredients of my identity, and a woman committed to racial and sexual freedom from oppression, I find I am constantly being encouraged to pluck out one aspect of myself and present this as a meaningful whole...but this is a destructive and fragmented way to live."

It can be helpful to think of your exploration as not necessarily about finding the right label, but about developing more authenticity. Being at peace with your self-identity encompasses your sexuality, along with your other identities, such as your role as mother, wife, or member of a community. All aspects of identity carry weight in decisions about transforming your life.

For a little while I thought I might have been gay, and I kept asking, "How do I know, how do I know?" But I came to realize that labels didn't matter and that my sexuality was fluid and that was okay. For a while, I was only attracted to women. Lately, I find myself very attracted to men. I even find myself fantasizing about gay men together. I try not to stress about whether to label myself as gay, straight, or bi. I just feel and love and live!
—EMMA

Is your sexual preference inborn, or is it a choice? According to historian Frederick Suppe in *Same Sex: Debating the Ethics, Science, and Culture of Homosexuality*, there have been over one thousand studies in the past century attempting to find the causes of homosexuality—that is, is it a result of a hormonal imbalance, a particular brain type or abnormality, birth order, parental characteristics, psychological dysfunction, etc.? The results of these studies are contradictory and often politically motivated. In short, research into the causes of homosexuality is inconclusive.

In my therapy practice, women seem to have divided opinions about whether sexual preference is a choice or hereditary. Many women who had some awareness of attractions at a young age or in adolescence feel that they had no choice about sexual identity, it was an inborn characteristic. Others, who have been attracted to the opposite sex for most of their lives and have an unexpected, sudden attraction to the same sex may think that there is choice involved. They often identify themselves as bisexual as they begin their exploration. If they lived somewhat happily with their husband, they may feel they have a choice. Since they have no history or context to fit their desire into, these new feelings sometimes have an unreal quality. After concerted efforts to understand themselves better, many women conclude that attractions aren't intentional. We can't control our attractions, but we can control what we do about them. Members of the Ask Joanne board often discuss their first attractions and how they used the information moving forward.

Lisa Diamond, author of *Sexual Fluidity,* suggests that we may have an intrinsic sexual orientation, but there is a lot of variability within the sexual labels we use. Her studies reveal that women's sexuality is often changeable and affected by the choices we make throughout our lives. We develop our sexuality based on both our inherent traits and the ways in which we interact with our environment and life events. These interactions are constantly changing, which explains why you might suddenly deviate from your normal pattern of behavior.

To understand your new awareness, it helps to look at what factors influenced or triggered your curiosity (falling in love with a woman, feeling dissatisfied with your sex life, feeling affected by a lesbian movie, etc.). Sexual fluidity doesn't necessarily mean you have a choice about whom you're attracted to, but you make choices all the time that may impact your sexual and emotional experiences. For instance, after eleven years of marriage I was restless and dissatisfied with my sex life. When I had an affair with a woman, I discovered what was missing in my marriage. The choice I made to get involved as I did led to new information. With that knowledge, I realized I wanted to explore my sexual identity. What was right for me in my early twenties no longer felt right in my early-thirties.

Most of today's discourse about human sexuality takes into account the context of our lives. Someone who lives an isolated life on a ranch in an ultra-conservative area of the country—like one of the characters in the movie *Brokeback Mountain*—may never pursue a same-sex attraction, or if they do, they may not identify themselves as gay or lesbian. If you grew up in a home with restrictive homophobic parents, you may have avoided acknowledging your attraction to girls. Later, at a more mature and self-reliant stage of life, you may suddenly open to your attractions and begin to follow a different path.

What Are the Components of Sexual Identity?

In the 1940s and 1950s, Alfred Kinsey conducted the most comprehensive study of sexual identity in the renowned Kinsey Report. His research found that people's sexual behavior, feelings, and thoughts often contradicted the way they labeled themselves. Both men and women had satisfying experiences with members of the same sex. People who defined themselves as heterosexual often had homosexual experiences at different points in their lives, and similarly, gay people had heterosexual experiences. The categories of sexual identity, he concluded, were indistinct. Some people who identified themselves as gay had never had a homosexual experience, and some who had been sexual with a member of the same sex didn't identify as gay. Liv's experience is a perfect example:

I had the most wonderful relationship with a woman for six years. I was seventeen years old at the time. It never even crossed my mind that I was lesbian. All I knew was that I loved this woman.
— LIV

I recall several years ago working with a woman who had been living with and sexual with another woman for five years. Neither of them defined themselves as lesbians. It wasn't until the relationship broke up that she began to question her sexual orientation. She had fallen into the romance with her friend, but now was faced with the question of whether she wanted to pursue intimacy with another woman or with a man. Her experience supports Kinsey's findings that people's sexual behavior sometimes differs from their fantasies or the way they identify themselves. In addition, most people don't fall into a distinct category of homosexual or heterosexual; they seem to have preferences that are not exclusive and that change at different points in life. While this idea was embedded in Kinsey's studies, only recently have sex researchers focused on the changing and flexible nature of women's sexuality. Given all the variables, there are no objective criteria for determining sexual identity; it is something that you need to establish for yourself.

The fact that many married women are still with men doesn't make us bisexual, because sexuality is a state of mind. If my heart and my head and my passions are with the women I love and want, I believe I am lesbian.

— ANGIE

Kinsey created a scale to evaluate sexuality. The scale is used for measuring to what degree we feel we are gay or straight for each category of sexuality. The categories include the following: whom you are attracted to, whom you have sexual fantasies about, whom you choose as sexual partners, whom you fall in love with, and how you choose to identify yourself, privately and publicly.

People often feel discomfort or lack of integration when there are tremendous discrepancies among the different categories. For example, some women may feel attracted to women and prefer relationships with women, and yet be uncomfortable with the sexual activity. There are many possible explanations for such discomfort. You may be generally uncomfortable with sex as a result of your upbringing or body image difficulties. Internalized homophobia could be interfering with your sexual enjoyment. Or, as revealed in April's message below, there may be specific techniques that are uncomfortable for you.

I am such a lesbian at heart, have known for a long time and have come OUT to everyone, etc., but I am having a great deal of difficulty enjoying lesbian sex. Because of some physical problems, I find making love to my woman is difficult, sometimes even painful. I don't like oral sex, and I feel like I disappoint my woman a lot. Sex with my husband felt much more comfortable. I very much enjoy the closeness, cuddling, and kissing with a woman, but when it comes to sex, it really is just so much easier with a man.

— APRIL

Many women feel that once they reach acceptance of their sexual identity, they should love sex with another woman. Sex can be difficult in heterosexual or gay relationships, and it isn't necessarily because we're identifying with the wrong sexual orientation or the wrong partner. A couples' therapist who knows about lesbian sexuality and relationships can help to resolve such problems. It is not unusual to have some struggles in the area of sex, regardless of sexual orientation.

When I was with my husband, I wasn't really afraid to try new things. I was so used to disconnecting and/or faking it that I didn't feel any pressure. Now that I'm with my girlfriend, I find myself having a harder time getting comfortable with trying new things in the bedroom, even though I actually enjoy the things I do with her. I don't get why I can't overcome those hang-ups. Is it because it's a new relationship and I am a shy person or is it performance anxiety or something else altogether?

— MARYLOU

April saw Marylou's message on the discussion board and shared her experience.

For the first time, it suddenly mattered to me that sex was good and that put pressure on my performance. I was scared to do something wrong since my girlfriend had always been gay, while I was "new to it all." It took some time for me to feel at ease with what we were doing (in terms of not getting it "wrong"). My girlfriend had to be very patient in explaining that there is no right or wrong!

— APRIL

Sexual anxieties can arise for many reasons, including past experiences, early messages received from our families, feelings about our bodies or particular sexual practices, etc. We may be excited and also uncomfortable with a new experience. It's not unusual to need some time to feel at ease with a new sexual partner. It's also not necessary to love all sexual practices. Most initial anxieties will eventually subside and the newness can add to the excitement about your unfolding sexuality. If you have found a loving partner, talking together about your concerns usually helps any issues.

How Do I Explore My Sexuality?

Some women feel strongly that their personal morality will not allow them to explore their sexuality while in a monogamous marriage. Women differ on how important it is to make love with a woman in order to know their sexual orientation.

Even if you have had a sexual experience with a woman, you may still be unclear about how to view your sexuality. It can be reassuring to remember that there are myriad variables that comprise sexual identity, which means that there are also many different ways to approach your exploration. The important thing to know is that such exploration will deepen your understanding of who you are.

Explore Your History of Attractions

If you never shared your feelings for women with anyone, those feelings may have begun to feel unreal. Without any validation of your experience, it can be hard to trust yourself. From a young age, we develop our sense of self, a belief in our experience of the world, through validation from parenting figures. Whether you suppressed or consciously hid your attractions to women, you may need to dig into the past to unearth an authentic sense of who you really are. In the message below, Amber wonders what is real and looks into her history for some answers:

Sometimes I think that I am making up all of these feelings. But then I look back over the years, even those of childhood, and I see that my feelings for females were there all along, but maybe not as intense as they seem to be now. I don't want to think that I've turned everyone's life upside down over "made up" feelings.

— AMBER

If you identified at one time as a lesbian and yet made a conscious decision to behave differently, that denial of your true sexuality may result in a struggle with depression. With growing maturity and introspection, some women discover they have created a mask for the world that they can no longer maintain. In the excerpt below, Marcia explains that she married on the rebound after she and a girlfriend split up.

I was so tired of being different, so I forced myself to date men. I met one who was nice; we married and have been together ever since. He is my best friend, but I now realize that although I can force myself to be straight, I don't enjoy it— it isn't working anymore.

— MARCIA

Your way of managing your attractions may have been far less conscious than Marcia's. Carrie is another woman who tried for years to avoid early lesbian feelings. She discovered that holding in something as significant as her sexual identity created a sense of shame. In my therapy practice I often work with women who, later in life, want to confront their fears about being gay in order to begin a more authentic life. I worked with Carrie in therapy to help her to overcome chronic depression. In her twenties, she believed marriage was her only option. Carrie felt intensely that she didn't want to be gay but found it increasingly difficult to deny her reality. Over the years, she avoided close relationships with women and any activities like sports that could possibly identify her "difference." When I saw her in her mid-thirties, Carrie was introverted and expressed low self-esteem. In order to address and possibly resolve these problems, she needed to find a way to integrate her sexuality with her personal values.

Bisexual is a misunderstood label, one that some women find easier to accept initially than lesbian. It may offer a sense of flexibility, more space for variability in their gender choice. You may have known about your feelings for both women and men, and chose to live in a heterosexual marriage, but are now questioning your choice. Lenore wrote to me, explaining that she feels something is missing in her emotional life with her husband:

I am forty-six years old, and have considered myself bisexual since about age thirteen. I had an affair with a woman once, but have not been with anyone but my husband since. I am finding that my desire for a woman is much stronger now that I am middle-aged. Am I feeling this as a physical or emotional desire? If I don't have anyone I'm interested in, then why such a strong desire at this time in my life?

— LENORE

Bisexual women often believe that their sexual expression involves choice, and midlife is a common time to examine choices. They usually find a different kind of fulfillment with men than with women. Lenore may feel it's important to experience more of the woman-identified part of her sexuality. Such awareness can be difficult because if you want to build a monogamous life with a partner, you will need to choose one way of life over another.

In *Two Lives to Lead: Bisexuality in Men and Women*, Fritz Klein found that many bisexual people feel that they are attracted to the qualities of particular people rather than aspects of gender per se. He also found that while bisexuals can be attracted to both sexes, they usually have a preference, and the preference may change back and forth over time.

Some women believe that the coming out process is more complicated for bisexuals than for lesbians. Joely is a married woman who has tried for several years to become comfortable with her bisexuality. She finds the label difficult enough to explain to her straight married friends, but was surprised at how disregarded and disbelieved she was by so many gays and lesbians. She had a hard time convincing people that she is not sitting on the fence, avoiding a gay or straight label. She doesn't believe she is confused, nor, she asserts, is she part of a "swingers" bisexual set, who maintain a lifestyle similar to the "hook-up" culture of college students. She is in a loving and supportive open marriage, one that allows for other relationships. Joely has been confronted by many of the myths our culture maintains about bisexuality.

- *People who define as bisexual are clinging to heterosexual privilege.*
- *Bisexuality is a phase that always ends in either heterosexuality or homosexuality.*
- *Bisexuals need to be with both men and women at the same time and therefore don't commit to one relationship.*

These myths don't hold true for most bisexuals, but there are instances in which the myths reflect some reality. Labeling oneself as bisexual can be one step in the process of becoming comfortable with a lesbian identity. For some, the bisexual label is temporary and for others it is a comfortable self-identity.

Is Your Attraction for One Woman or for Women in General?

When you fall in love with a woman for the first time, you might imagine that it's
an isolated experience or you may think it's a sexual orientation issue. Frequently, such exploration takes place after the end of a love affair, when you're free to pay attention to whether you are attracted to other women. If you are currently romantically involved, you may not be able to answer this question. but if you're not, you might start by noticing who catches your eye when you walk down the street. What qualities are you attracted to? A type of appearance, the way someone moves, a personality type, gentleness, self-assurance?

Rachel's experience illustrates the dichotomy between feeling an attraction to just one woman, as opposed to women in general:

> *My girlfriend is married and has fantasized about women in the past. I am her first "real" experience with female love. She confessed that if her husband and I were "gone," she would pursue a female relationship. She now questions why she married her husband and why she never has gotten really close with female friends before. I, who never used to fantasize about women and would probably stay with men if she were "gone," am the one who sees our life together so easily. She is terrified to change her life, yet I am not. Is there a hidden meaning in her reaction versus my reaction?*
> — RACHEL

Rachel's girlfriend is facing a sexual identity issue. She knows her preference would be for women if she weren't married and she is afraid to face the confusion one might naturally feel when facing a core identity shift. Separating from her husband would force her to deal with her struggles about being gay. Rachel is not experiencing a change in her sexual identity because she believes that her attraction is for her girlfriend only.

Over time, as two women begin to build a life together, other identity questions are likely to arise. How long can Rachel be with a woman and continue to feel that she is not lesbian? If they develop a friendship network with other coupled women, will they be viewed as lesbians? Her self-definition may change over time.

Should You Seek Out Women?

I fell hard for a woman a year ago. There is no hope of a relationship. Having just about worked through the shock and guilt, do I actively go searching for someone else and in the process hurt so many people? It seems that accidentally finding someone is a different thing from an active search.

— BRIDGETTE

It's impossible to deny what you are doing when you begin to actively search for other women. This situation can create severe guilt, and it is not an easy undertaking. Single women are often reluctant to get involved with a married woman, so many married women specifically seek other married women when searching for lesbian experiences.

You may choose to understand yourself better without being sexually unfaithful to your husband, which is why some women pursue activities and events that bring them in contact with lesbians. As long as you stay open to your feelings, you can learn about yourself by getting to know other women who love women. There is more in Chapter 9, "Expanding Your Support and Resources," about ways to expand your resources toward the goal of developing self-awareness. If you are committed to fidelity, you may need to leave some questions about your sexual identity unresolved as long as you remain married. Yet even women who have had a relationship with a woman may have unanswered questions that only time and self-exploration will resolve. You can move your personal inquiry along by developing a keen awareness of your feelings and reactions to people and experiences. Becoming mindful of your emotional and physical responses may be all that's necessary for you to know the right path.

When I compare my visceral sexual feelings when thinking about sex/intimacy with a woman or watching The L-Word and fantasizing to my thirty-nine years of life when I really wanted to feel that intensity but never did with men ... that tells me I'm gay.

—VERNA

A bi-curious/sexual person doesn't have such a dramatic inequity of natural sexual desire. Thoughts of being with a woman make my head want to explode and I'm almost drunk with desire.... I've always wanted to feel that way for my husband and, historically, with men, but never did. I had the desire to have the desire but never felt it.

—ALLIE

Is This a Phase?

Some women fear that they may make an enormous life change only to discover that their attraction to women was just a phase. It may help to keep in mind that our lives consist of various phases and that we move in and out of life stages. It is important to give yourself enough time to determine the importance of this phase.

Is it possible to have loved your husband at the time you married and to have even had a fulfilling marriage until this current phase?

If you felt satisfied, you needn't rewrite your history or recall only the things that were missing in your marriage. Of course, some marriages have been unhappy, but if you were relatively content, there are other ways to view the metamorphosis. For much of my marriage, I felt generally satisfied, even happy, but in many ways, I didn't know myself. As I developed more self-awareness, what I wanted from a partner and from life changed. My husband did not grow in the same way. As I began to learn more about my sexuality, I changed in ways that were irreconcilable. This time of self-reflection can reveal unforeseen issues. You will need to decide for yourself whether the changes that you desire are possible with your husband. Trish shared a lovely way that she and her husband, while still living together, reminded themselves of the better times of their marriage:

> *We're putting up a scroll in the house where we'll write down the things that are good about US, the good memories, etc., to honor the marriage we've had, so we can release each other but also validate the ten-plus years we've been together. We're beginning to talk of this as a successful (not a failed) marriage that just ran its course for the time in our lives that we needed it.*
> — TRISH

Given the complexity of human sexuality, your interests and desires can change at different times. It would be inappropriate to view your current same-sex attractions as mistakes. They are real. What is open to question is their importance to your identity and your choices surrounding them. A woman who was separated from her husband and living with her lover for close to a year asked, "If one turns into a lesbian, can that process be reversed, turning back into a heterosexual wife? For the sake of the kids, for the sake of the job, for the sake of the dream of a home I always had?"

Her unspoken question is: *Are my decisions reversible?* One potential answer is that almost anything is possible. Lesbianism or heterosexuality are more than sexual acts or even attractions to a particular sex. Both orientations involve a decision. One doesn't "turn into" a lesbian. It is much more likely that this woman simply began to honor sexual feelings that are a part of her. Yet she still has to consider the other aspects of herself and to honor her values. Only then will her life decisions bring her complete fulfillment. This discussion board participant's experience is instructive for all of us: it's best to hold off on decision-making until you can be confident that you will be at peace whether or not the marriage doors are closed.

How Do You Know If You Can Be Happier?

Some women have never had a positive experience with another woman. As a result, they have nothing to compare to their current marital relationship. In fact, I hear from some women who are quite unhappy with their lesbian experimentation. Regina writes about her confusion; she thinks she knows what she wants, but doesn't really know if it is possible. She may not be able to answer her question as long as she remains married and truly unavailable.

I can't figure out whether I am a lesbian or not. I've been rejected by both women and men. My husband knows what's going on with me and still wants our relationship. I have no desire to sleep with him and he doesn't seem to care. I have guys stare and flirt with me, but I have no desire to flirt back. I just want to treat a female like I want to be treated.

— REGINA

Another woman, Sandra, tells me she is getting close to identifying herself as a lesbian who is married. Yet she still doubts her ability to be happier or more successful in any other relationship. Sandra has had a distant, contentious relationship with her husband for more than twenty years and is quite aware of her own contribution to the problems. The several affairs she has had with women over the course of her marriage have been more intimate, but just as volatile. Sandra concluded that she must have intimacy problems.

That may be the case, but it is important to consider other factors. Any married woman who becomes emotionally and sexually involved with a woman is facing the stresses that any affair brings. Because the extramarital relationship is formed in a stressful context, it takes a leap of faith to believe that the relationship could be calm and happy under different circumstances. Those women who are involved in unhappy marriages are often afraid that they are not able to truly love the way others seem to love. The truth is that you can't know for sure if you will be happier in a relationship with a woman. But what you *can* know incontrovertibly is that you are unhappy. Once you are able to trust your awareness, you can then address the causes of your dissatisfaction.

The Coming-Out Process

Social theorists have described how the initial confusion and loss of a sense of self experienced by people exploring their sexuality can be attributed to predictable stages of the coming-out process. While the older models of coming out don't focus on the natural fluidity of women's sexuality, they can help you see some common themes of coming out. Vivienne Cass's coming-out model, described by Warren J. Blumenfeld and Diane Raymond in *Looking at Gay and Lesbian Life,* is a good representation of several difl models. While recognizing that every individual is unique in her process, Cass's model depicts a general pattern that includes six interconnected and non-linear stages. Your initial attraction or sexual involvement with a woman usually takes you to the first stage of this coming-out process. If you decide somewhere in this process that what you are experiencing is not a sexual reorientation, you may end your exploration at that point. No matter how you ultimately define yourself, the stages of most coming-out models lead to the reintegration of your sexual identity with your overall personality.

Stage 1: Identity Confusion. Most people feel confused when they first notice an attraction to someone of the same sex. This early stage of initial recognition often leads to a sense of alienation. You may have thought you knew yourself and your life's trajectory, but now your existence becomes defined by an overriding question: "Who am I?" Usually these feelings remain secret because of shame, fear, and ambivalence.

I am still attracted to my husband physically, yet I consider myself to be woman-identified and crave the emotional connection that I'd hope to find with a woman. I've never had a physical affair with a woman, so I'm wondering if I'm really bisexual or lesbian or just a person who's having a mid-life crisis? I'm confused.

— TIFFANY

I'm presenting a picture of myself that isn't really me - i.e. typical happily married wife/mother - and yet I'm not sure who I am, and can't really introduce myself to people as "married, oh but, by the way, also questioning my sexual identity and whether I love my husband."

— KARIN

I can't figure out how I've gone from loving sex with my husband to not enjoying it at all. Does that mean I've fallen out of love with him, can't handle having a husband and a girlfriend emotionally, what??

— JOSLYN

Stage 2: Identity Comparison. You may find yourself trying to rationalize or find a plausible explanation for anything other than being gay in this second stage. Common statements during this stage include, "I could be lesbian, or maybe I'm just bisexual." "Maybe this is just temporary." "Perhaps this love is just for this one woman." "This is about loving a person—her gender is irrelevant." During this stage, women often feel totally alone as if no one else has experienced what they are feeling. While it's true that in the media today there is increasing discussion about the phenomenon of coming out later in life, it's still common for women to believe that no one in their circle of friends would understand. This belief may be true for some women, based on their local environment, while for others it's based more on lingering fears.

The following thoughts that have appeared on my "Ask Joanne" board are quite common during this stage:

- *Since I am married, I realize that I have been rationalizing my first lesbian crush by telling myself that it was "safer" than having a crush on a man.*
- *I know that sometimes we can desire a deeper emotional connection with our spouses and when that is not met we tend to reach for it in someone else.*
- *I've never known real passion before women; I never really knew what attraction was all about, but then I wonder if it is just the novelty of things.*

- *I started acknowledging my attraction to other women shortly after finding out my mother was diagnosed with cancer. It has been a long, painful year and she just passed away last month. So I'm worried that my obsession with lesbian movies, books, and online lesbian sites was just a means to distract myself from my grief.*

Stage 3: Identity Tolerance. Once you start taking action, you have entered the third stage. In this stage women begin to accept that they may be lesbian or bisexual. You might take actions such as confronting your isolation by looking for other bi or lesbian women, seeking counseling, or choosing a few trusted friends or family members to share information about your sexuality. While you may not embrace a non-heterosexual identity, you begin to develop a sense of tolerance. I began to attend meetings at a local lesbian organization, which was quite active at the time I came out. Although I felt like a fraud (because I wasn't really a lesbian, I thought), I wanted to meet other women who did identify as lesbian. In fact, that's where I first met my life partner.

I've been coming out to myself for about four years now. At first, I thought that I was bisexual, but the more I find out about ME, I'm realizing that I'm lesbian. At first, I thought that I would never break up my family. But the more time goes by, I'm feeling more and more caged up, frustrated, unhappy, and miserable. I've just recently realized that I cannot stay in my current situation and I don't want to. Now I just feel the need to reach out.
— MARGUERITE

Stage 4: Identity Acceptance. In this stage, women begin not only to accept their new identity but to form friendships with other women who identify as lesbian or bisexual. Depending upon your age and the political culture of your home environment, you may use different terminology to express your non-heterosexual identity. You may adopt the label of "queer," or "gay," or some other term that acknowledges your love for women. Some people never reach acceptance of their identity. They may know they are gay, but continue to hide this awareness from most other people.

Accepting and embracing myself has been one of the most wonderful things about this whole process. My husband and I have separated, something I never would have imagined a year ago. Having supportive, positive reactions from gay and straight friends has been incredibly helpful as I start coming out to people. There have been some negative ones, too, but I just have to remember that I am not responsible for others' emotions.

— LILLIE

I am making friends with women in my community and discovering a connection with other women "like me." Finally, after all of these years, I notice that when I see a woman I find attractive I don't immediately feel shame about it or hear the voice in my head say, "You can't think those thoughts."

— SHARISE

Stage 5: Identity Pride. Women in this stage begin to feel a sense of belonging to this new community and a shared sense of being an outsider. They increasingly come out to other people and become immersed in the lesbian culture. Women often feel angry about heterosexual privilege and the loss of their human rights, such as the freedom to hold a partner's hand in public, the right to bring a partner to a family gathering, or to know that their children won't be taken from them because of their sexual orientation. I learned the hard way and felt very resentful that I suddenly had to think about the political/social environment of any place I was planning to vacation with my lover. I discovered that being in a homophobic environment was not relaxing or conducive to having an intimate romantic time. Like many other women, I too was angry and worried about the potential cruelty from peers that was often acceptable in my kids' school environment. I had a tendency at this stage of my coming out process to slam people who didn't see homophobia or recognize the homophobia inherent in their comments. My reactive responses changed gradually as I integrated my sexual identity into my total sense of self.

> *The first years after separating from my husband, I went to the local lesbian bar with my girlfriend and attended as many women's music festivals as I could. I volunteered at a gay and lesbian mental health center and learned about the community by hearing from many different lesbian clients. I came out with a vengeance at graduate school, expressing anger at anyone who didn't understand the oppression of our underclass. This was definitely a phase—a very passionate one.*
>
> —IDA

Stage 6: Identity Synthesis. In this stage, women integrate their sexuality into the rest of their identity. There is still a sense of pride, but less anger and less of a dichotomy between the heterosexual and homosexual worlds. I personally learned to turn my anger into action by explaining homophobia to friends who didn't recognize it and by using my profession to help women feel pride in taking a stand for who they are regardless of potential negative reactions.

I'm getting comfortable being alone and getting to know myself again. I have finally gained both a bit of patience and a sense of comfort with the unknowns in life. The future is no longer scary as I spend more time in the present. And I realize I've made more friends—both gay and straight—in the past year than I have in the past ten. I have become so open and happy that people are suddenly drawn to me. Fun, fun.

—DANA

The anger of the Identity Pride stage is considered by some to be less mature or integrated than is the Synthesis stage. However, many believe the anger in the former stage is an appropriate end point, in that it confers legitimacy on those who choose political activism regarding the inequities of our culture. You may be happily ensconced in the Identity Pride stage, or you may be more comfortable approaching those whose ideological approach differs from your own with less anger and more openness to dialogue.

Again, these stages are not necessarily linear. For instance, a sense of alienation may reflect an early stage of the coming out process, but it also can become a pervasive experience throughout life even after fully identifying yourself as lesbian. Or you may begin to take action, as described in Cass's Stage Three, which may cause you to revert to Stage One, feeling confused and even more ambivalent.

This coming out model is only a guideline. For example, Cass suggests that a woman who feels her attraction to one woman is a one-time experience is in the early stage of coming out. However, Paulita's message below shows that being attracted to only one woman was just that, an attraction to a person, not a shift in her sexual identity.

When I experienced physical intimacy with my lover, it felt wonderful. At that point, I looked around and tried to figure out if it was just her I wanted or if I wanted to be with other women as well. For me, it was just her. It was then that I turned the corner to give my marriage a chance. I wanted that intimacy from my husband.

— PAULITA

No one but you can identify your sexual orientation. Because you have to live with yourself—because you have to live in your own body and with your own spirit—you are the one who must determine what is right for you. As you work on clearing away societal and/or family expectations, you will begin to recognize and access your true feelings. You will be coming home to yourself.

Straight people don't stay up hours at night debating if they are gay. The amount of sadness and discomfort that comes from not living life as your truest best self is damaging to you and everyone in your family. We each must do what our hearts know to be true.

— ROSLYN

WHAT YOU CAN DO NOW

Remind yourself: Self-understanding is not a linear process. You may take one step backward for every two steps forward.

Ask yourself this question: What messages about sexuality, direct or covert, did you get from your parents, teachers, clergy, and friends? And which do you continue to hold inside?

Practice this technique for handling anxiety: Keep your focus on the present. Focusing on the past tends to lead to depression, while focusing on the future can overwhelm you and promote anxiety. Problem-solve only for the current issues. This you can manage.

Take one step: In daily life, it is important to keep your focus on the present. However, exploring your personal history can be vital in developing insights. Make a timeline of the key sexual events in your life. How did each of these events affect your life? How did they shape your thoughts about your sexuality? Identify thoughts you would like to challenge.

CHAPTER 3

EXAMINING YOUR MARRIAGE

Do You Want to Save Your Marriage?

This is the first—and most critical—question that every married woman faces when she has questions about her sexual identity. By the time women contact me with questions about their sexual identity, the majority have already fallen in love. If you are currently involved with a woman, emotionally or physically, consider the following. Your new relationship is likely to have its own disappointments as the intensity fades. Is your romantic involvement more than a distraction from difficulties in your marriage, or is it a transformative experience? Do you know whether you are facing a question of sexual orientation? Would you regret leaving your marriage if your current relationship ended? Or if another relationship weren't available? There is no guarantee that if you leave your husband for a particular woman, your new relationship will last. Much is at risk, and you want to know that you can live with your decisions. It may help to identify what you are seeking and whether there is a possibility that you can find it in your marriage.

A new sexual experience or an exciting affair may be a distraction from the deep-seated problems of your marriage. However, this is the perfect time for you to examine the strengths and weaknesses of your relationship with your husband. Affairs or extramarital interests often occur when something isn't quite right in the marriage. If the marriage equilibrium is already upset, you may be more motivated to examine the causes and potential remedies in order to return balance to your life.

Evaluate the Strengths and Weaknesses of Your Marriage

After thirty-one years of marriage, I have been digging deep inside to find out why I am unhappy. My husband is kind and I love him like a brother. Yet there is no intimacy in our relationship, and that is something I really crave. I feel no sexual attraction to him, but I don't look forward to hurting him.

—IRENE

Many women who contact me report that their husbands are loving and supportive even after learning about their wives' attraction to women. These men may have a strong initial reaction, but seem willing to wait to see what will happen, wanting what is best for their wife. Like Irene, you may have no extraordinary problems or obvious reasons for your unhappiness, nothing you can point to that is wrong with your marriage. Your husband may love you, and be a good provider. Perhaps you have fun together and feel that he knows you well. As Irene told me, "The only things I miss in our relationship are the feeling of closeness and good sex." In response, I pointed out, "It's no wonder you're unhappy, because these are two of the most essential aspects of relationship satisfaction." There are some who believe that leaving a spouse would be less difficult if he were abusive, but this may be simplistic thinking. Many abused women are fearful of their husband's reaction if they were to try to leave.

I've been asking for many years that we spend more time together and talk more openly about "feelings," among other things. This desire to have more emotional intimacy has increased significantly over the past number of years for me to the point that I've realized I can't have this with him.

— CLARISSA

Married women mention desire for more emotional intimacy so frequently that it appears to be a pivotal issue. Women often find that intimacy with a man is quite different than with a woman. An experience of intimacy is so individual that you will need to explore this for yourself. Clarissa voiced her concern: "I want to be in a partnership with someone I can have different levels of intimacy with. Am I being unrealistic in this desire to have more emotional intimacy and a 'true' partnership?"

Examining the possibility for more intimacy in your primary relationship can be so complicated that it may require a dramatic change. Clarissa decided to move out to learn more about her sexuality and to address the intimacy question. She felt she could no longer stay in her marriage at such a cost to herself. She was lonely with her husband and had a painful longing. She had been responsible and respectful of others, often at her own expense. If you are a caretaker, like Clarissa, try to find an opportunity for solitude to learn about yourself. It may be time to ask, *What about me?*

Are you harboring a long list of complaints about your husband? Your anger at your spouse may actually hinder the careful self-scrutiny required to discover what is truly causing your unhappiness. Liz understood this only after she separated from her husband:

I realized I'd been angry that he never heard me tell him how difficult it was to live with a person who took me for granted, who was never at home (a serious workaholic), and who didn't want to connect on an emotional level. It took him three years and a separation, but he finally gets it, and it really released me. Validation is so incredibly important. Now that I don't have that omnipresent anger at my partner in life, I'm able to focus on the other reason we separated . . . my attraction to women.

— LIZ

Why Now?

As you begin to review your marriage, pay attention to the timing of your exploration. Gina, for example, began to explore her bisexuality within the first two years of her marriage:

I have been bi-curious for YEARS, even before our relationship. While I was always too scared, it wasn't until after I married that I felt mature enough to explore my sexuality. I'm twenty-six; my hubby of two years is forty. I don't want to hurt anyone, but I don't want to sit on the sideline and always wonder about myself. How can I spread my wings without knockin' him in the head with them?

— GINA

There are critical points in marriage that demand increased levels of commitment. It is actually common to begin your sexual questioning at these times, when you are deciding whether to take the next step. One of the tasks early in marriage is to become comfortable with a deeper level of commitment. To achieve this, loyalty must be transferred from the family of origin to the new family you create with your spouse. This shift usually happens in the first two to four years of marriage. However, it's difficult to cultivate the trust and safety of the marital bond while embarking on a new exploration of your sexuality.

If you are in the early stage of marriage, it will help to take the time, before getting too deeply into your search, to examine your marriage. You may begin by asking yourself these questions: What are the most important qualities that you desire in a life partner? Can you create the kind of marriage with your husband that will bring you enough happiness? Do you want to be with him? If you do, it may be time to focus on settling into your marriage and creating the necessary trust and communication. An extramarital relationship at this time will distract you from working on the problem areas of your marriage. Marital work may help to answer the questions above.

Other important junctures that demand increased commitment include decisions to buy a house, have a baby, change careers, move to a new location, handle a loved one's death, etc. Women have joined my support groups while pregnant, remodeling their home, entering graduate school, or looking for a vacation home with their spouse. For married women, it appears that these pivotal events occur simultaneously with their sexual awakening too often to be pure coincidence. Each event represents both transition and additional commitment to the marriage—a fertile time for self-questioning.

If your sexual exploration revolves around a current romance, you face an additional dilemma: How can you compare the excitement and novelty of an affair to everyday pressures and familiarity of a longstanding marriage? You might ask yourself whether you ever had similar feelings for your spouse. Are you experiencing something that seems very new to you? Eventually the day-to-day problems seep into any relationship. Is there something qualitatively different about this new relationship with a woman? The last question is one of the key markers I explore when women feel confused about the meaning of an affair. If they feel that the level of excitement and intimacy is similar in their extramarital relationship to what they felt when they first became involved with their husband, I would encourage them to work on their marriage to discover if it's possible to bring back some of those qualities. A qualitative difference might signal a sexual orientation issue, especially if they've never had the same experience with a man.

Talking to Your Husband

Feelings of guilt, avoidance of conflict, and fear of consequences may all play a part in your reluctance to talk to your husband. Just knowing that a lot of people could be hurt often prompts naturally honest women to think about keeping secrets. Some maintain their secrecy, but there is a price to pay: many people have trouble living with secrets. It is difficult logistically to remember the lies, and it can be hard on self-respect and on the integrity of the marriage. Your decision regarding whether or not to talk honestly is very much connected to the degree of openness and honesty you have had in your marriage prior to this transitional time. In some marriages there appears to be a covert agreement not to talk about things that may lead to rupturing the marital bonds. Your decision about how much to discuss may also relate to your family and cultural background.

Many women have written to me regarding their fears.

How do you tell the person who loves you so much that you don't feel the same way and that, in all reality, you're attracted to women, not men? I'm consumed with guilt and feel that I've completely let him down. I know I need to tell him, but how do I even begin?

— MAGGIE

I don't want to be stupid when I talk to him. I do NOT want to lose custody of my two preteen kids. If I let him know, I might lose the comfortable life I have. He will be so angry with me.

— SAMANTHA

I do not want to break up our home, as we have a wonderful son, who I cannot even think about traumatizing. I'm afraid if my husband knew, he would not be willing to stay married. I'm not ready to face that possibility.

— JUDITH

I am happier than I can remember being for a long time since getting involved with a close friend. I love my husband, but I realize that I have spent my life trying to make sure he was satisfied, not realizing that my needs were not being met. I can't imagine ever being honest with my husband, but I can't imagine my future without her, either. I've always taken the honesty-is-the-best-policy approach, but there are a lot of people who could be hurt, and who have a lot to lose in this situation. Is it possible to live and continue with this secret?

— KATHY

If you are already involved with another woman, there is generally conflict ahead with your husband, with your lover, with your internal battles. If you don't talk to your husband about it, you stand the chance that he will find out on his own. If you keep the relationship with your girlfriend secret for too long, thus maintaining "affair" status, your girlfriend may tire of waiting.

When you feel paralyzed by fear of the potential consequences of talking to your husband, it may help to remind yourself that any skills you develop now can only benefit the outcome of this transitional time, whether you recommit to your marriage or leave it. Early in the process of sharing with my husband, I was unable to hold my own in disagreements. He always stayed so calm and rational. I gradually learned how to talk about the important issues without crying or becoming reactive to his words. We both needed to learn how to communicate better so we could continue to co-parent our two daughters.

If you are just awakening to your love for women, it is natural to keep your thoughts to yourself. There is so much to figure out. When you are ready, it makes sense to talk first to people who are less affected by your changes than your immediate marital family. You may wonder when, if ever, it becomes crucial to tell your husband the truth? Consider Ally's situation:

I've been coming out to myself for about four years now. I am realizing that I am lesbian. At first, I thought I would never break up my family. But the more time goes by, I'm feeling more and more caged up, frustrated, unhappy, and miserable. I realize that I cannot stay in my current situation and don't want to.

— ALLY

Ally's husband is very concerned about her because he sees that she is going through something "really big." Ally thinks he might suspect what it is, but she hasn't said anything to him and has started to pull away from him.

Like Ally, you may need to consider the impact of silence. Ally's husband is witnessing her distress but is rendered helpless by not knowing for certain what is creating her pain. Much of Ally's avoidance is due to the fear of hurting her husband. If fear is guiding your silence, read Chapter 4, "Husbands' Responses," for tips on confronting fear. It helps to anticipate all possible responses from your husband in preparation for an important discussion with him. Try to trust your instincts, keeping in mind that you probably know your husband and his attitudes better than anyone else does. When I was working out my decisions about whether or not to stay in my marriage, friends who were trying to be helpful warned me of the possible custody battles that might occur because of my love for a woman. I had heard stories about some grandparents who had tried to get custody in similar situations. When I was able to directly confront my worst fears, I realized that my husband had hired a very liberal, gay-friendly attorney to represent him. He wasn't going to use the "lesbian issue" to hurt me. I knew he thought I was a good parent and that didn't change over the course of our eventual separation. Looking more realistically at my husband as a person and at our relationship helped to assuage my fears.

Your desire to avoid an open discussion may go beyond your fear of hurting others. Many people are generally afraid of change. You may be hanging on to the status quo at a great cost to yourself. If you want to work through your fear of change, try to challenge your assumptions. Carol, for instance, wrote:

> My husband's pride would be crushed if I told him about my girlfriend, and I am afraid of what he would do to me if I left him. I stay for the well-being of my children and myself.
> — CAROL

She began to change her attitude by confronting each of her assumptions: Does her husband's hurt pride mean he won't recover? Is her life with her husband the only formula for her children's and her own well-being? You, too, may discover that your fear leads you to imagine the worst possible outcomes. It is helpful to stay aware of all possibilities. Furthermore, when you develop a more positive

LIVING TWO LIVES

attitude, you often unconsciously promote a better response from your husband.

Talking about your current situation is scary, but it is a terrible emotional and psychological burden to hold secrets or to try to plan for your future in isolation. When you open discussion, you may actually feel less guilty because your husband will now know and have the option to plan for his future. If you tell him the truth—about your struggle and how much you don't want to hurt him or let him down—he may be able to see beyond his own pain. Let him know your feelings and your concern for him. Hopefully, you will remain caring and sensitive about each other as you negotiate your lives, both together and separately.

While there is pain involved with honest discussion, it may help your husband to talk about his fears. Eventually, he will be relieved to know exactly what he is facing. He then can take some time to evaluate what he needs to do for himself. Ryan, one husband, posted this on my website (www.lavendervisions.com):

> The longer you wait, the more you will hurt your husband. I watched my family die like it was being eaten away by a slow cancer. Be honest with your husband. You owe him that much.
>
> — RYAN

Loosening Your Control

You may fear a spiraling loss of control if you reveal too much. When life is chaotic, the most basic human instinct is to hold on tightly. You try to control whatever you can. Perhaps you are not telling your husband where you are going, how you are feeling about your marriage, or the changes that you are facing. Some women begin to plan how to financially manage two households, where they will live if they move out, and what the custody arrangements should be long before any discussion with their husbands. An open discussion with your husband may feel terrifying. You may not even understand why you are controlling information. When your thoughts and plans stay only in your mind, you maintain the illusion of control.

As soon as you talk openly with your husband, you lose some control over what happens. Your husband may be suspicious every time you go out. He may become more controlling of your actions or demand more information than you are ready to reveal. While this increased involvement on the part of husbands may create new tensions, the communication usually helps the process of discovery to progress. Beth offered this important insight:

> When I find myself frozen about talking to my husband, I know something is holding me back. I must respect those feelings, even when I can't specifically identify them. I realize that I am terrified of losing control of the marriage. Even though my secret is eating me up, it isn't as horrible as the potential consequences I envision. That means I'm not ready. I need to be stronger inside myself.
>
> — BETH

You may believe that you need to know exactly what you want for yourself before you discuss the issues with your husband. While it helps to know your goals when entering a difficult discussion or negotiation, it could be a long time before your needs and desires are clear. Taking as much time as you need to clarify what you want is appropriate. Discussions often need to take place before you have answered all of your questions. As difficult as it may be, try to practice the art of letting go. Talk without having a script, without knowing how your husband will respond, without fully understanding yourself. Consider what you know about your husband in order to best prepare yourself for his responses. Abusive or excessively angry husbands require a very specific approach (see Chapter 4, "Husbands' Responses").

When deciding how much to reveal to your husband, you also should consider the possibility that the situation could become far worse. Not all husbands are understanding. Donna's message illustrates how the control of decisions can be yanked from you in some situations:

My husband was not understanding. He would not leave the family home nor would he allow me to stay there as anything other than a sexually submissive wife. I ended up being literally thrown out (for being a lesbian—although he used different terms to describe me!). It was not an experience I would wish on anyone. However, even with all that transpired when I told him the truth, I do not regret my decision for one minute.

— DONNA

How Much Should You Tell?

I just don't know how to approach my husband. How do I express to him that I think he is a great guy but that I need to be with a woman?

— PAT

Most women have the right words inside themselves. However, if you're at a loss, there are a number of good books (see Index: Resources) that discuss ways of coming out. A good place to start can be found right in Pat's message: Tell your husband that you think he's a great guy but you need to be with a woman. Let him know that it is not his fault, even if there are some marriage problems. It may help him to know something about your process. Most of all, communicate your concern for him.

If what you are revealing is completely new information, your husband is likely to have questions: Are you are involved with someone? How long have you been thinking about this? Did you know this before you got married? The more you can tell him, without going into great detail, the better it will help him to understand.

The initial and subsequent discussions generally go more smoothly if you are not self-deprecating. Most women feel guilty, but it is important to find compassion for yourself in this discussion. You might explain that even when women have some awareness of same-sex attractions before marriage, they make their choices based on their ability to handle those issues at that time. This concept applies no matter when you began to develop your insight.

It is more important that you speak to your husband than what you say. You might let your husband know that you would never choose to hurt him, but you need to follow a different path to be true to yourself and to him, and you want him to have the opportunity to be with someone who can give him the full love that he deserves. If you are unable to imagine letting him go or seeing him with another woman, then you may not be ready for this discussion. You may never have this discussion if your decision is to recommit to your marriage.

Speaking with sensitivity, giving useful information, and being patient are all important. Women often find themselves unable to move in any direction, mired in conflict in their attempts to get their husbands to understand. Your husband may never understand. His complete understanding cannot be your goal if you wish to move forward. He may have to come to his own understanding in his own time.

There are some general rules for the "big" discussions: Do your best to tell your husband the truth, talking to him in terms he can understand, and sparing him any details that might add to his pain. Try to separate your relationship problems with him from the experience you've had with a woman. Remember, you're just opening the opportunity to talk about what is going on. If you don't want to conspire with his denial, you need to give him enough information to know the truth of what he is facing

When you begin to reveal your same-sex attractions, it is unfair and unwise to expect your husband to be your confidante or primary support. As Jill wrote:

I discovered my attraction to women and have acted on it twice. My husband knows and is generally supportive, but also hurt and apprehensive. He asked me for details after a recent date during which I spent the night with the woman. How should I deal with these questions? I am reluctant to tell all for fear that he will become even more hurt and scared.

—JILL

The details would be very painful for almost any husband to hear, yet many husbands in such a situation need to talk about it. What they imagine is usually worse than reality. It is common for a husband to express his anxiety by obsessing about details. However, this still doesn't mean that you should discuss with him what you and your girlfriend "do" together. A marriage counselor can be very helpful in this type of situation.

You might be more inclined to share details if you are attracted to someone but have not actually had an affair. Jan, for instance, has fallen in love with a colleague with whom she has not yet shared her feelings. She told her husband everything:

Sometimes we talk about her—it seems so crazy for him to be talking to me about a girl that I am in love with. I don't think this is good for him, though. I feel physically sick most of the time. I feel so guilty I can hardly look at my husband. He still very much

loves me and says I should do what will make me happy. But he still expects me to act like a loving wife to him—which is hard.

— JAN

Beginning to Think Separately

It is a challenge to hold on to your feelings when you start to talk openly with your spouse. If your role in the marriage has been that of nurturer and caregiver, you may try to support and soothe your husband. The focus then shifts from self-examination to managing your husband's distress. Mindy described her struggle upon telling her husband:

When I came out and told my husband that I was involved with a woman and that I now realized that being with a woman was the right thing for me, he had a total breakdown. He cried day and night for a week. I tried to be as supportive as I could be, but then I just couldn't give anymore because I was also going through it myself. My husband didn't have any friends that he could call up to talk to. I proceeded to contact people who might be willing to support him.

— MINDY

Mindy's intentions were kind, but she will eventually need to encourage her husband to find his own support. At this juncture, you and your husband must discover independently what does or doesn't work as circumstances change. For real growth to occur, you may both need to develop parts of yourselves that you have abdicated to each other. For example, Mindy's husband, like most people, has areas in his life that are underdeveloped. In his search to find the right path for himself, he may discover the importance of establishing a greater support system. Perhaps he has relied too much on his wife alone for support.

Because your discovery and subsequent discussions are the source of your husband's pain, you may slide back and attempt to avoid the truth in an effort to make him feel better. Sometimes the truth hurts. The purpose of open discussions is to bring the truth forward so that constructive decisions can be made. Each partner needs to know the other's truth, even when it is painful. Timing, choice of words, and the determination of how much information to give must be considered throughout this process. Such choices can make a difference in how reactive or chaotic your marriage becomes.

Sexual Communication with Your Husband

I am feeling more and more awkward with my husband in terms of intimacy. He is still fighting to save the relationship. Part of his efforts involve being constantly physical with me— hugs, kisses, hauling me off to the bedroom. While I enjoy the physical comfort of his hugs, it is getting increasingly difficult for me to be any more intimate than that. On his down days, he gets very frustrated with the lack of passion or response from me, and this usually leads to an argument of some sort.

— SERENA

Sexual communication is often a metaphor for the general communication in marriage. What happens in your sexual relationship often mirrors the general dynamics of the relationship. Serena's husband may be testing her feelings about him by constantly pushing for sex. Direct communication is important in sexual expression, as well as in discussion. When you just go along with your husband, you perpetuate his denial. If you have sex when you really don't want to, you are not only deceiving him but betraying your own body. Husbands sometimes use sexual responsiveness as a way to reassure themselves that everything is okay.

Sexual difficulties with your husband during this time may not be just about sexual preference. For most women sexual openness is not just physical but relates to feelings of affection for their partner. You may be avoiding sex with your husband since discovering a new level of intimacy with a woman. If you have been distant from your husband, it makes sense for you to feel less sexual. One decision you face is whether to try to improve your sexual responsiveness with your husband. Paradoxically, improvement will generally require more open communication in the other parts of the marriage.

Your decision to stay or to leave your marriage depends on your conclusion after examining your belief systems. You may decide to stay in your marriage because you love the life you have, not because of love for your husband alone. If you recognize this decision as a choice, you are less likely to feel resentful. Sacrificing yourself for the welfare of your family may be a consideration, but you cannot save others if you are denying yourself a satisfying life. Your denied desires are usually communicated in some form, such as irritability, low energy, or depression. It may help to determine whether you can recapture the joys of life if you work on maintaining the marriage.

When I walked into that church to marry, I did so because of the immense love I had then (and still do) for my husband. Whether people believe that or not "quite frankly I don't give a damn," because only I truly know what is in my heart then and still is now. Guilt has been the hardest thing to deal with. But I'm working on it. I'm sorry that this process takes so long, but it is complicated.
— JAN

WHAT YOU CAN DO NOW

Remind yourself: You honor yourself and your husband by taking the time necessary to evaluate the marriage, whether or not a sexual identity issue is involved.

Ask yourself this question: Do I have the will and desire to continue to work on my marriage?

Practice this technique for handling anxiety: If you are ruminating about the future or the past, put a rubber band around your wrist, and every time your thoughts take you away from the present, snap the rubber band. Ask yourself: What is it I need to be doing right now?

Take one step: If you have not told your husband about your attraction to women, make a list of everything that stands in the way of that discussion. Try not to censor anything. Knowing your fears is the first step toward addressing them. If you have been talking about this issue, tell your husband one new thing about what you are facing. This helps both of you to break through any denial, avoiding the dishonesty that comes from omission.

CHAPTER 4

HUSBANDS' RESPONSES

Husbands often go through a predictable process when learning about their wives' sexual exploration. There are several noticeable phases they go through, not necessarily in any particular order. Your husband's initial response can be heartbreaking, especially if he expresses his sadness openly. It may help to remind yourself how long you have been dealing with your discovery, yet this is completely new to your husband. Depending on your husband's personality, you may witness responses ranging from tears to a blank stare or, in some cases, violence. Disbelief is another common initial response. It often takes him time to allow the reality of your situation to seep in.

You may observe him vacillating between denial and the other phases (bargaining, anger, and facing reality) that potentially lead to acceptance. Even after your husband begins to realize the seriousness of the situation, he may latch on to any sign of change in you that offers him a sense of relief. If you disabuse him of his hopes, he may become angry. It is important for your husband, just as it has been for you, to work his way through the range of emotions that he encounters so that he can move forward and rebuild his life. You may find it challenging to allow him this part of his healing process and to avoid the impulse to appease him.

Nina describes her husband's struggle on the "Ask Joanne" internet message board. Even after two years of knowing the truth, her husband continues to cycle through different phases: depression, model husband, anger, apathy, and back to depression. Tamika writes about the same topic: "My husband has vacillated wildly between trying to be the perfect husband and being extremely verbally abusive when frustrated or feeling that his efforts aren't having the intended effect." Both women discovered that there is no set timetable or linear process that spouses traverse to reach acceptance.

The Phases

Denial

I came out to my husband a few months ago now. I felt a great rush of relief (and excitement and fear and . . .) but tick, tock, tick, tock; time is passing and NOTHING IS HAPPENING. My husband and I don't talk about it. I feel as if I struggled to lift a very large rock, threw it into the pond, caused enormous waves that subsided into ripples, and now the pond surface is calm again.

— GERRY

After the truth has been revealed to husbands, denial is often their most persistent and implacable defense. This may be expressed in many different ways. Gerry's husband has tucked away the news. If she doesn't talk about it again, it's as if the discussion never happened. Some husbands may just not believe that this is a real issue, or they think this can't be happening— it's probably just a phase, not a serious problem. In some cases a husband may even find it titillating to imagine his wife with another woman.

It's possible to unwittingly support your husband's denial if you are not giving him enough information.

My husband knows the issues I'm dealing with but believes that it is a part of menopause. Denial is a great thing.

— SUZIE

Suzie wrote that in her gut she knows that her marriage is not going to work out happily ever after. She asked me how long it usually takes for a couple to realize it's time to separate. Her husband has known about her situation for about four or five months. In fact, that length of time is relatively brief in the overall scheme of life. Suzie is considering a major move that involves many changes. She told her husband about her girlfriend, and now she is waiting for something to happen. You, too, may be stuck in a holding pattern, expecting your husband to take the lead. If your husband goes into denial, as many do, waiting for your husband to make a move can feel endless.

In addition, his denial places you in the position of either choosing to go along with him to keep the peace, thus colluding in some kind of lie, or constantly reminding him that you aren't happy. When your husband is in denial, you have to bring up the subject and keep the discussions alive. One husband shared his experience:

She told me she was gay. I said I knew this, but it really wasn't obvious to me until she said it. That's when I really knew, or at least accepted what had been right in front of me all this time.

— STEPHEN

If you are exploring your attraction to women, it's possible your husband has been living with less than all of you for a while, but he has probably not mentioned it as a problem. Since you are the one who's feeling unhappy with the status quo, you will need to initiate the changes. By accepting that responsibility, you challenge both yourself and your spouse to face reality and to learn how to speak directly and honestly to each other. Denial is so common that you may need to bring the topic up again and again with gentle reminders, such as, "We need to look at this," or, "I still have these feelings and I am working on myself," or, "How are you handling the information I told you?"

Bargaining

When faced with a traumatic loss of this kind, many husbands offer immediate but unsustainable solutions. Some men become the perfect husband, making all the changes that their wife has ever wanted. If they are perfect enough, they think, she may decide to stay with him. Kerry's husband is responding to his potential loss by bargaining with her.

> *I love my husband so much, but I just don't feel whole and complete with him since coming out. He knows everything about me but is hopeful that we can stay together and have our own girlfriends. It is hard for me to imagine this. I just don't know if I can continue to live together with him as best friends instead of husband and wife. I don't want to do anything to hurt him. I just feel that things would be better if I moved out and started over.*
> — **KERRY**

Bargaining is a common response when a husband first learns about his wife's sexual exploration. You may feel a new, helpful, but maddening support from your husband. He is putting his own feelings on the back burner if he listens to your tales of heartbreak and even makes suggestions regarding meeting women or managing your love life. While this appears to be what a wife would want, this kind of response usually precedes the husband's true examination of his feelings and the possible consequences of his wife's attractions. Support from your husband is likely to make you feel guilty when what you are expecting is his anger and resentment.

In his attempt to be helpful, your husband may also become enmeshed in your exploration. If you have turned to your husband for advice in many parts of your life, it will feel difficult to break out of this pattern. Florence, for instance, had revered her husband, often trusting his perspective more than her own on childrearing as well as work-related issues. As she moved through the process of clarifying her sexual identity and becoming certain about her desire to be with a woman, she projected a date for leaving her marriage. Her husband, Steve, kept finding reasons why it would be bad timing for the kids or for his job. He discouraged her from talking to the kids about their planned separation as well as her sexuality, despite signs that the kids were wondering about their parents' changed behavior.

You will find that in this discovery process you may need to learn how to let go of the constant focus or reliance on your spouse and begin to think more independently. If this sounds familiar, you and your husband will need to redirect attention to your own feelings and beliefs and learn to trust yourselves more. As you begin to speak out about your ideas and opinions for handling the changes, your husband will be challenged to let go of his control and take your suggestions more seriously. This eventually should help you to become more self-reliant.

Anger

Even if your husband is supportive, he may become angry once he faces the true meaning of your revelation. When it is apparent that the sexual identity issues are not going away, some husbands have angry outbursts or become very withdrawn and distant.

> *When the bargaining/denial stopped, anger took over. This was after I had left. He would not consider sharing custody of our girls (ages seven and ten.) This sweet man that I had been with my whole adult life was ready to slander me so that he would get custody. I NEVER thought it would come to that. Every conversation was hurtful. "You are ruining fifty people's lives with this 'decision' for YOUR happiness," he would say.*
>
> — PATRICIA

Patricia's husband reverted to his old, supportive self again when he began to accept that the divorce was final. He realized that there was nothing he could do to keep her, and that she was a much happier person "not with him." Your husband's anger may be partly related to his feelings of helplessness—there is nothing he can do to change the situation. Once he is able to accept your changes and he stops trying to fight the situation or fix it, he is likely to feel less angry.

After their initial shock and dismay, as I have mentioned, most husbands try to be supportive. However, some men are not so understanding.

> *I was wondering if anyone's husband has had negative reactions. I have young children, and my husband is extremely homophobic. I'm afraid he will do anything he can to take them away from me if I ever come out to him.*
>
> — MARY ANN

If you have any suspicion of a potential custody battle, as in Mary Ann's situation, it may be best not to let your husband know about your exploration before you talk to a lawyer. Each state and each county has its own attitudes and even prejudices. While it makes no sense ethically, if you live in an area that is very conservative, you can actually lose a custody battle based on sexual orientation. A knowledgeable attorney can help you to know your legal rights and to determine the degree of homophobia in a regional court system.

Facing Reality

Husbands have their own grieving to do. They are facing a loss, even if the marriage continues. They have new information that affects their sense of security and causes them to question what they thought they knew about their wives and their marriages. The marriage may survive, and may even eventually improve, but it will never be the same. As husbands face reality, they usually assess more honestly their own feelings and beliefs. Sadness is a necessary part of this process. Your husband must bring the focus back to himself to discover what he needs from the marriage and what these changes will mean to his future.

Once I REALLY understood, fear set in. I realized then that there is a good chance I will lose her as my wife. The pain of that was nearly unbearable. After my realization, much of what I went through is just a blur. It was an emotional maelstrom of fear, pain, anger, rejection, and all that fun stuff. I cried. I cried for the loss of what once was, I cried out of fear of what was to be, I cried for our children, I cried for my wife, but most of all, I cried for me. My demons had found me.

— JAMES

Acceptance

Men often have a hard time revealing their marital struggles to others. Part of your husband's journey toward acceptance involves expanding his support system. Husbands often find that they have relied on their wives for their primary support, and under these new circumstances, they cannot continue to do this. As husbands start to share their stories, with a professional, a close friend, or a family member, they may find that they are able to focus their energy on the decisions they must make. Your husband, like you, needs to make his own choices about how he wants to live. There are books, organizations, and websites that can offer support to your husband.

I love my wife. Wherever her journey may take her, I will always love her. I can only hope that her path will lead her back into my arms again, but whatever the outcome, she needn't worry about me. I will be okay and so will she.

— TIM

Special Circumstances

If Your Husband Is Abusive or Threatening

In this case, the previous sections of this chapter do not apply to you. Once you understand what constitutes abuse and recognize that you have an abusive husband, there are specific actions you need to take to protect yourself and your children.

If you are repeatedly being controlled, influenced, intimidated, or threatened by your husband, you are dealing with domestic violence. Most importantly, there does not need to be physical violence present in order to be in an unhealthy relationship. Repeated emotional abuse is also considered a type of violence. If you cannot act in ways that you would want because of fear of retribution by your husband, your relationship is unhealthy. Establishing safety supersedes any other planning for now.

Your husband is abusive if he has a pattern of any of the following behaviors:

- *Threats of violence or violent behaviors*
- *Threats of suicide as manipulation*
- *Loss of temper or intimidating rage*
- *Verbal or physical abuse of your children*
- *Abuse of your pets*
- *Demeaning behaviors directed at you*
- *Obsessive possessiveness or jealousy*
- *Use of finances to control your actions*
- *Use of sex as an act of aggression*

Honesty is not the best policy for handling an abusive husband. You should have a plan of action before you even let him know that you are unhappy with him. Your plan may include police or court-ordered protection, preparations for leaving at a moment's notice, and a place where you can go with your children. Safety preparations should also be developed with your children, such as going to a safe space during an argument, going to a neighbor's house, and knowing phone numbers to call for help, etc. Children are generally aware of the abusive relationship even if they don't physically witness the arguments or abuse.

In most cities, there are agencies that will provide legal help and/or counseling, as well as safe shelters for you and your kids, if necessary. Whether or not you follow through, it is important that you be informed of your legal rights.

My husband is a loaded gun. He is a difficult man with impulsive control issues. The marriage is not a good one. So, do I leave on that premise, or do I tell him I am gay and leave on that?

— CARA

When trying to determine how much to tell your husband, you must take into account what you know about him. If he has been abusive or vindictive before, he will likely respond that way. I told Cara that her personal safety and the dissolution of the marriage is the first priority. At the time of separation, you need to be very cautious about how much you reveal. It's best to extricate yourself from the marriage based on marital problems without discussing any of your questions about your sexuality. Above all, you need to minimize the potential for further abuse or revenge.

It may become necessary for your husband to know more at a later time if you have kids, because it's hard to ask children to keep a secret that will become burdensome to them. Once there is some distance from the conflict of separation, if he continues to share parenting responsibilities and if he is less volatile, it may become safe enough to tell him the added truth.

The thing that I am most afraid of is the backlash that could come from me splitting up with my husband. His pride would be crushed, and I am afraid of what he would do to me and to our children. I am stuck here, afraid to leave, for that reason.

— LETREESE

Letreese is in a frightening situation. I suggested that she contact a lawyer to determine her legal rights. If you, like Letreese, are maintaining your marriage out of fear, try to look at the larger picture. Children who observe domestic abuse are more likely to re-experience it in their future adult relationships. It is important to help your children understand that they are witnessing abuse, in terms appropriate for their level of development. Angry husbands do a lot of blaming. Your children may misconstrue the backlash directed at you for leaving or for coming out. They may not recognize that you are leaving because of your husband's behavior. This may be your opportunity to offer them an experience of intimacy that is different from the kind of interactions they have observed between you and your husband.

My husband divorced me when he found out that I was in love and having an affair with a woman. He has always been abusive, and he made sure that I suffered as much during the divorce proceedings as I did during the marriage. He copied my private emails to my girlfriend and sent them to family and others. Since our divorce, he has told everyone we know that I am a lesbian and cheater. My life is horrible. I never know what he will do next.

— MADELINE

Unfortunately, as I pointed out to Madeline, an abusive husband will be an abusive ex. You may need help in learning how to confront his behavior. As a first step, stay away from your husband and have as little contact as possible. The best way to handle rumors and bad-mouthing is to try to stay in contact with the people you love, and who understand your situation. They won't want to hear him speak negatively about you. In this kind of situation, it is best to stay in contact with friends and others who can offer support. If you continue to feel threatened by your husband, it's time to contact the police and/or a lawyer.

Safety is the most important concern, and your belief and understanding of your husband's capability for abuse are the most important indicators. Learn to trust your abilities and reach out for support. Being involved in an abusive relationship can be incredibly isolating if your spouse is able to maintain control based on the isolation. Remember, it is not your fault.

If you are involved with an abusive man, you may also encounter abuse in your relationship with a woman. The forces that cause abuse in relationships are complex and require careful examination. Before you move into a new relationship, take time to understand the ways you learned to cope with abuse; a knowledgeable therapist can help you to create new strategies. Whatever you learn now will lay the groundwork for a better future.

If Your Husband Is III

Normally it is difficult to evaluate your marriage, or any other aspect of your life, while you are caught up in the passion of an extramarital relationship. This situation is exacerbated if your spouse is suffering from a serious illness.

My husband was diagnosed with stomach cancer seven years ago. Our sex life diminished, and my feelings for women grew to the point that I thought of nothing else. I did not leave him because I felt it my obligation to care for him. But this whole time, I look, want, NEED, and think only of women and the life that is just slipping by as I sit here and watch. How can I leave a man who is very ill and has no one else but me? How do I stay in a life that's not mine only because I can't handle all of the guilt?
— CHARLENE

At age forty-nine, Charlene began to look at her marriage to better understand herself and her paralysis. Her husband has a terminal illness but could live for another five or ten years, with increasing special needs. When a husband becomes ill or needs special care, your decisions are more ethically charged. If you are the primary caregiver, you may feel that your decision comes down to his life versus yours. Can you or should you sacrifice your happiness to do what you believe you must do?

As Charlene struggled with this dilemma, she became terribly depressed whenever she focused on her husband. She was resentful of the time she devoted to taking care of his physical needs. Eventually she reached some resolution. She continued to take care of her husband and to covertly, rather than openly, involve herself with another married woman who was unable to leave her marriage. Both were satisfied with a part-time, closeted relationship for the time being.

If your husband requires health-related care, try to find ways to balance your needs with his. You may find, however, that the ongoing "sacrifice" is not sustainable—that it is not enough for you to find some happiness "on the side." Ultimately you must examine your marriage, and there are many factors to consider when doing this. If your husband has just a brief time to live, that will affect your decision. However, some women feel we are given one life to live, and they want to live it in a way that is meaningful and fulfilling. In this case, you may decide to confront the situation with your husband honestly and face the facts. It may be difficult to help your husband to live a happier, more peaceful life if you are miserable in the process.

If You Have a Chronic Illness

I feel very trapped, unsettled, and sad. Seven years ago, I was diagnosed with MS. Single lesbians don't want to talk about it with me, straight friends want me to stay with my husband, and I just want to run away.

— CAROLINE

If you are disabled or living with a chronic illness, you may be more dependent on your husband than are other married women.

This makes sense if you have had an expectation that your husband would be the one to take care of you as your illness progressed. You may have the same questions and concerns as other married women, but you also face uncertainty about who will be there to lean on when your health deteriorates. Moving from a known situation into an unknown presents far more risks. If you have a girlfriend, the awareness that a first relationship often doesn't survive the married woman's entire journey takes on added significance. You need to explore options for assistance that you never examined before. Like other women with special concerns, you must weigh your future security against your ability to find a happy enough life while you are still relatively healthy. As you consider all the factors, keep in mind that future security for all of us is relative. No one really knows what the future will bring. What is most important is that your internal, subjective experience of security is adequate.

Mental Illness

Most women whose husbands supported them through a difficult mental illness feel a sense of gratitude and obligation. When you have emotional problems, your instability affects the marriage. As with any debilitating illness, you need to look at your ability to take care of yourself. If you depend on your husband for emotional help, for economic security, or for primary childrearing responsibilities, it is especially important to evaluate your means of support as part of your decision-making. Learn what your illness requires and use that to anticipate the kinds of support you will need if you leave your husband.

A Note to Husbands

Whether you suspected something had changed or you are taken fully by surprise, the news of your wife's exploration surely sends you into crisis. If you feel that your marriage has enough history and richness to help you wait this out, you may need support to do so. There are books and websites that give information and help for spouses in your situation (see Index: Resources). Try to open yourself to asking for help. A gay-friendly, knowledgeable therapist of your own can provide guidance at this time. It is frustrating and difficult to maintain clarity about your feelings when you know so much is at risk. A therapist can help you stay focused on yourself and what you need.

Offering compassion during your wife's struggle provides her comfort, but don't get sidetracked from your own questions and decisions. How long are you willing or able to wait? Do you want to work on the marriage? Can you make changes that may help your relationship? If your wife is truly facing an issue of sexual orientation, what do you want to do? What are your limits and boundaries for a fulfilling marriage?

Even when it is uncomfortable, it's important to talk about what is happening. When you have questions, ask your wife. However, it won't help either of you if you constantly probe. You have every right to feel mistrust and insecurity. Trust will need to be reestablished. If your marriage is to survive, it will take time to repair the feelings of betrayal. The particulars of your situation will determine in part how feasible it is to try to rebuild your marriage. Of course, you are not in control of the outcome any more than your wife is. This factor may be the most frustrating part of your new situation. During this time, create some projects and activities that you might enjoy. You can use this time to identify what you need for a fulfilling relationship. Authenticity for both you and your wife is the foundation for a happy marriage.

WHAT YOU CAN DO NOW

Remind Yourself: Your husband's response is a grief experience. Recognize the limits of your ability to be his anchor.

Ask yourself this question: Am I giving my husband enough information to promote honest dialogue?

Practice this technique for handling feelings: When you feel drawn into your husband's struggle, carve out twenty minutes without outside interruptions to answer these questions: Where am I stuck? What stops me from moving forward?

Take one step: It is important to respect your husband's process and honor his responses. However, it is crucial to keep a focus on yourself and necessary decisions. In order to do this, you need to set boundaries. Define your limits regarding:

- *Listening to his anger, sadness, or fear.*
- *Responding to his questions.*
- *Tolerating his silence.*

CHAPTER 5

MANAGING THE ROLLER COASTER

I feel as if I'm giving birth to myself, feeling young, vulnerable, raw, exposed. It's as though my life is going through such a dramatic shift, that at times it's too much to bear. My husband and I have gone through a myriad of emotions together (anger, sadness, acceptance, back to anger, relief). In a given hour, I go from feeling excited, calm, and so bloody sure of myself to feeling hopeless and scared.

— JULIE

Julie's description may sound familiar to you. Women often compare their journey to a ride on an emotional roller coaster. You have a sense of euphoria when you first experience a new kind of love or an aspect of yourself that has until now remained hidden. Then, as you begin to face the meaning of your feelings, or get caught up in lies and deception, you may feel anxious, reactive, confused, frustrated with your confusion, overwhelmed, and guilty. In short, the whirlwind of changing emotions throws you into crisis.

This is a time of rapid change—changes in events, in the people who share your life, in your feelings and beliefs, and in where you focus your attention. You may be suddenly paying attention ions that have long been repressed. If you have fallen in love with a woman, you face numerous unexpected questions. If your love is unexpressed or unrequited, a longing emerges that can become a painful obsession. If you are having an extramarital affair, you must deal with your lover's emotions, your husband's reactions, and your children's responses to the shifting emotional environment. These sudden changes affect your emotional, physical, and spiritual well-being. Nevertheless, this roller coaster ride is a normal and necessary part of your discovery process. The ride will eventually slow down and clarity will return.

Highs and Lows

The woman I love has always identified herself as lesbian. It was over a year before we realized that there would be anything else for us but our wonderful friendship. I am very much in love with her. Passion, fire, laughter, caring— all that is present. My hope is to be brave enough to stop living this double life at some point.

— SHEILA

Falling in love is exhilarating. The intense feelings that you have may be your first true romantic attraction. Most women step onto the roller coaster because of such glorious feelings. Sheila describes the energy and heat of her new love. Some women also feel a sense of freedom as they step outside their normal life. One woman described "feeling alive" for the first time in a long time, perhaps ever. She didn't realize that she had been numb for years until she finally found the courage to reveal her attraction to the woman who subsequently became her lover. Even with all the craziness that accompanied her ride, she realized that she never wanted to return to her feeling of deadness.

You, on the other hand, may not have stepped outside the typical patterns of your life in the eyes of the world. Many women go through dramatic changes all internally. Sonya, for instance, told me:

About a year ago I became involved in a professional relationship with a woman who I am undeniably in love with now. She may think that I have some type of crush on her, but I have never told her anything directly. I'm not certain what will ever become of this situation. But it has opened a door in my life that I can't shut.

—SONYA

Sonya's internal experience of attraction and romance is as consuming as an affair. Her fantasies are exciting, and the moments of close contact with her colleague are her high points. The resulting sense of guilt and confusion is just as strong as if her emotional ride were visible to others. Sonya had experienced prior attractions, but had found this too scary to confront. She now has more self-confidence, and no longer wants to deny her attractions.

However, Sonya doesn't want to pay the cost for a roller coaster ride in the real world. She holds her turmoil inside herself. You may be like Sonya, who tends to be cautious. You may get nauseated just imagining the ups and downs of the roller coaster. If you generally avoid risks or are very fearful of change, you may choose to keep yourself on solid ground, at least on the surface. Taking a step that could unravel the structure of your current life may present too much danger for you. It might feel safer to keep your struggles silent and play out the possibilities in your mind. This may be as far as you go. On the other hand, your internal musings may be preparation for making the ride more manageable.

The charged excitement of this awakening is closely associated with fear. Most people feel anxious when they do something different or act out of character. On this journey, your once predictable life no longer seems certain. When you know what to expect, even when it's painful, you can prepare yourself. On this ride, you enter unfamiliar territory; so many people are affected, and are influencing your choices, that you are unlikely to steady your course quickly. You must learn to tolerate the experience of not knowing: not knowing what to do, what will happen, what direction to take. This loss of certainty is often the most difficult part of the journey.

It is ironic that the rush of excitement and anticipation is what may catapult you into despair and fear when you face the reality of your marriage. You have some choice about how you handle your attractions, but your family is inevitably pulled along, and they didn't make this choice. Throughout this process, I thought my guilt would lie with the affair, but I have dragged someone else into this part of my life. Instead of sorting out what was going on with me, I moved forward and got married to a great guy to see if I could ignore my feelings and see/hope it would work. I feel guilty that I have misled him.

— MARTA

Depending on when you first began to look at your sexual orientation, your feelings of guilt will have a different focus. If you had an early awareness of your attraction to women, like Marta, you may blame yourself for not working through your areas of confusion before marriage. You will need to work this through to bring your attention to the present. If your awareness developed after you married, your feelings may focus primarily on your infidelity. Sheila reveals the inevitable conflict and despair that accompanies the euphoria of an affair:

I spend my evenings at home trying to act like everything is okay, when all my thoughts are of my lover and when I can hold and touch her next. I still am sexually involved with my husband, but there are times when I want to scream and not let him touch me, yet I feel an obligation to meet his needs. I am spiritually battling with the fact that I'm having an affair, more than the fact that it is a lesbian relationship. I'm committing adultery.

— SHEILA

Lies and Deception

The majority of women I have counseled have not been dishonest with their husbands prior to their sexual awakening. Yet most women in this transition find themselves caught up in a web of deceit, either lying or omitting the truth. Like Sheila, you may find that your dishonesty undermines your personal values, spiritual beliefs, and, ultimately, self-esteem.

Lying requires a lot of energy—you must remember what you have said and learn how to lie convincingly. When you feel guilty, it is difficult to be convincing about the things you're trying to hide. The resulting stress can reach a breaking point. Many women unconsciously leave clues around that suggest an underlying desire to have the truth uncovered. They may forget to delete an email message from a lover or leave their personal journal around, inviting the scrutiny of a curious or suspicious husband.. The upheaval often comes when husbands discover an affair or some other deception. This puts you back on the roller coaster with new levels of highs and lows. Everyone involved, including your girlfriend, goes into crisis mode. Discovery usually initiates reactive anger and tears, demands, promises, and broken promises.

I don't like having a secret, and it's eating me up inside, but I'm scared to do anything about it. I figure I have so much to lose. I am so confused again, just when I thought I was doing better. It still comes down to the "Should I tell or not?" "Should I stay or not?" "Should I talk or push it down?"

— MURIEL

When you have no one to talk to, your thoughts and feelings tend to become circular and unresolved. Yet it is natural to wait until you find the right words to explain what you feel. However, you should question whether your silence is a means of avoiding feelings of fear or shame.

Reactivity

My depression is all-encompassing. Just when I think I know what my decision should be, my feelings change. One minute I want to leave him to be with her. Then I think, how could I ever get past it? He has made so many changes. He lets me be me. He just wants to have babies and forget this all happened. It is a terrible position. I feel so much guilt, so much pain. My town is small, my reputation is ruined, my husband is wrecked.

— CONNIE

Often women make decisions prematurely. In fact, it is best to avoid making any major decisions during a time of upheaval. There are several reasons for this. You may be reacting to your inability to tolerate the uncertainty, the painful experience of not knowing. Or, if you are used to keeping the peace in your relationships, you may be responding to pressure from your husband, lover, or family primarily to avoid conflict. If you make decisions that are reactive or premature, you may unconsciously undermine the outcome. If you don't take an action that you unconsciously desire, you may covertly upset the status quo. In her message, Leigh anticipates this possibility:

> *I don't want to sit on the sidelines and always wonder about myself. I am afraid if I don't learn about my sexuality, then I might leave my husband, or create tension to make him leave me.*
>
> — LEIGH

Another woman named Anita decided to separate from her husband after one difficult week of conflict. She found an apartment nearby, but when she moved in, she felt uncomfortable in the small space and was extremely lonely. Anita continued to have regular contact with her husband and began to feel a pull to mollify his sadness. In less than two months, she returned home. Anita wasn't fully ready for her decision. In addition, she was unprepared for her emotional reaction to her husband's neediness. A major move of this kind requires a good amount of planning, and anticipation of the areas of support needed so that you can successfully adjust to your changing situation.

> *Almost six months ago, I started questioning my feelings when I fell in love with a woman. We became so inseparable that I moved out of my home and in with her. My husband is crushed. There are so many emotions with this and kids involved, and I am depressed over it all. I can't be happy, and I'm not sure how I can be in this situation when I don't want to hurt anyone. I am so torn, because I can't have both and don't know what to do and can't live like this. How do I go about making such a life-altering decision and feel no guilt and at peace and happy with myself, because right now it is killing me inside?*
>
> — MARSHA

Experiencing the emotions that follow your actions may be the best way to learn what it is you want. Note your feelings, but try not to act on them in any way that causes major upheaval in your life and the life of your family. Giving yourself sufficient time to consider the issues and the repercussions will generally create less dramatic upheaval, both for yourself and your loved ones.

> *I know that each and every time I tell him that I realize I am gay, and it has been countless times now . . . I get stuck when he sobs, and stuck when he has temper tantrums, and stuck when he calls me at her house because he is suicidal. You have to know what you will do when and if that happens. Or you will be like me and you will wait two years to try to tell the truth all over again.*
>
> — ABBY

Abby may have been able to stay her course more successfully if she had more distance, either emotionally or physically, from her husband. If your husband knows what you are facing and you two are living together, you may be reactive to his emotions and he to yours. This is a torturous but normal part of your transition. There are some suggestions at the end of this chapter to lift you out of this quagmire.

Know Your Feelings

Emotions are valuable guides when you are trying to make decisions. You may have learned to ignore your feelings as a way to block out pain. Some people learn not to trust their feelings. They often have higher regard for the opinions of others. When seeking your truth, you cannot rely solely on other people's advice. Feelings indicate your comfort level with your thoughts and behaviors. They help you to become more conscious of areas of conflict and direct your attention to the issues that need work. Pay attention to your feelings of joy and love, as well, because all emotions are helpful guides to mind-body-spiritual integration, and thus authenticity.

Grief and Depression

After my lover left town, I fell into a deep depression that lasted for three months. This was a new kind of love I had to reckon with. Eventually the grief helped me understand that I wanted to have this new emotional depth as part of my future, and that information enabled me to make my decisions. You too will need to fasten your seat belt and stay on the roller coaster until you understand your feelings and allow them to help you.

There is much to grieve in this process: the loss of your marriage as you knew it, and of yourself as you have understood your identity or the image you have projected. It can be helpful to make a list of your losses. You may be grieving the ending of your first lesbian romance. Your list should include those things, tangible and intangible, that you have already lost. When you get into "potential" loss, you're moving from sadness into a different emotion—anxiety. When you focus on future concerns, you are worrying about something that hasn't yet happened, and may not. You need to keep yourself focused on the present in order to resolve problems.

Right now it is important to acknowledge your losses so that your sadness has a clear context. Life will get better as you move through your grief. Grief has stages that are similar to husbands' processes described in Chapter 4, "Husbands' Responses": denial, bargaining, anger, letting go, and acceptance. Working through grief takes time and is essential to your moving forward and letting go of your past.

Fear

Are you afraid to move in any direction? If you have tried something new or made a small decision and then found yourself retreating, even regressing, fear may be guiding you. When you allow yourself to stay with the free-floating fear, you are more likely to uncover the specific concerns that need your attention. This is not easy to do, because people often develop coping mechanisms that shut off or avoid fear. These defenses include constant activity, addictions, and focus on other people to the exclusion of yourself. I know I sometimes work long hours, watch television, or grab something to eat when I am upset. Try making your own list of ways that you avoid your fears.

There are days when I say to myself, "It's time to move forward," and that scares the hell out of me. Then I ask myself, what really deep down scares me the most? Is it being alone, or the financial insecurity that will mean a serious lifestyle change? Or that my kids might shut me out, my husband will not only be hurt but damaged forever, the hometown gossip, or that the traditions and family dynamics will change drastically?

— BETTY

Betty's process for managing her fears offers some important tips. When you address each fear separately, it's easier to assess how realistic it is. Most of Betty's fears were exaggerations. You may find, as she did, that you are capable of handling each of your concerns. Through her process, Betty could see more clearly that her reason for maintaining the status quo was to save everyone else. She wrote, "I suppose I am giving up my life for them once again."

If you want to identify your current fears, try an exercise I use in my support groups. Using a free-association approach, try not to censor anything, and write what comes to mind quickly (too much thought will encourage you to evaluate and censor). Make a list of everything that you are afraid of: everything from rejection, loss of your children, to being a lesbian (and what that entails for you), or what it would mean if you discover that you are not gay. Let your mind take you in as many directions as it can when identifying your fears. When your fears are examined separately, they become more manageable. You can then look at them individually, evaluate how real they are, and begin to develop the courage and skills to handle them.

Guilt and Shame

In a workshop I recently attended, a participant offered one way to differentiate between guilt and shame. Shame, she suggested, is the sense of disapproval and embarrassment about *who you are*; guilt involves the same self-assessment, but is about *something you have done*. Both feelings are common for married women on this journey. Although there have been dramatic changes in societal attitudes, there continues to be a cultural norm in many places that instills homophobia. When you consider engaging in homosexual behavior, you may feel shame at times. You might know intellectually that it's okay to be gay but have deep feelings that it is wrong. Even if you have always held a liberal perspective about the right to be gay, you may stumble on unexpected feelings of disgust about a sexual experience or discomfort when you first see two women dancing or kissing. For some women, it takes time to become comfortable in such new and unfamiliar situations. It helps to be in the company of lesbians to overcome the cultural stereotypes that affect us all.

Your feelings of guilt are often related to the pain you think you're inflicting on the people you love. They may be associated with being secretive or inattentive to your children. There are many opportunities to feel guilty. Most of us have some positive guilt that helps guide us in making decisions that take others into consideration. However, if you allow your guilty feelings to overshadow all else, they will not be helpful in this journey and may impede your progress. To address these feelings, try to talk to yourself from a rational perspective. For example, when facing guilt about hurting your husband, you might remind yourself that you are trying to find a solution that will ultimately make life better for both of you. One of you can't be authentically happy if the other one isn't. It is appropriate to feel sad about hurting your husband.

If you have a lot of guilt from the past, you're more likely to feel overwhelmed by feelings of guilt now. In this case, a therapist could help you understand and move through your guilt. You must take into account the nature of your marriage, as well as your husband's true nature, to fully understand that you can't take responsibility for "destroying" his life. Only he can do that. If your feelings are appropriate to the present situation, you will eventually find a way to accept this new reality, and recognize that if your husband is reasonably healthy, he will survive, and possibly grow and benefit in the long run.

If your guilt is about not living up to someone else's standards, whether the standards of your family, church, or society, it may be time for you to determine a standard that is right for you. At some point, it becomes important to work toward developing your own principles and realize that it is impossible to please everyone. This time of life is ultimately about discovering your authentic self. You may need to consider breaking away from old standards that no longer apply to the person you are becoming.

Anger

Whether or not you recognize it, anger is a part of all relationships. This is especially true when you are disrupting the status quo. Sometimes it's easier to identify other people's anger, or your fear about them getting angry, than to look at your own. If you follow society's gender models, you may hide your anger from others and even from yourself. You may not feel that you have a right to be angry at this time because guilt frequently masks anger. You may have had grievances and annoyances during the course of your marriage yet hardly be aware of anger at your husband now. Sometimes it's easier to identify your sadness, fear, or guilt. However, anger is a part of this awakening process, whether it's direct or indirect, and it needs to be examined.

Anger doesn't necessarily make sense. It often has no rational basis. You may be angry at your husband for not providing the intimacy you desire. Your rational voice says, "I'm the one who has changed, he has always been like this." Or your anger may be focused on the way he is so accommodating and supportive, making the situation even more difficult for you. How can you be angry at him for being nice? You may be frustrated that he won't make a decision. Part of you knows that he is just as confused and scared as you are. You could ask him to change his behaviors, but really, are you angry that he can't meet your needs the way a woman can?

It's important to dig deep for the underlying causes of your anger and be tough with yourself about it. Anger can be a projection onto your husband of the frustrations you feel toward yourself. For instance, you may want him to make a decision that you find hard to make. Instead, you blame him for being passive. Perhaps you are angry that he isn't initiating discussions. Take an honest look: are you too afraid to bring up the difficult topics yourself?

At times, anger can be helpful. It makes separation easier, whether physical or emotional. Anger creates the distance between you and your husband that may help you move apart. I hear from women who know they want to leave their husbands but focus only on their love or gratitude toward them. These women often feel completely stuck. If you are trying to separate, anger may give you energy to take the action. If you are not planning to separate physically, you still may need more time away from him to clarify your own position.

This is a tender time. Some women have regrets about how they handled themselves during their transition. Serious damage can occur to you and your family when you don't handle your anger appropriately. You can control only your part of the conflict, but there is a lot you can do toward this effort.

It's important to express your anger in a direct and thoughtful manner. If you become certain that your anger is not about him, you need to stop the charade of blame. You will develop more clarity if you can communicate your feelings to others. It may help to talk to a friend or a professional to defuse your anger before bringing up issues with your husband. This is a good time to talk to an understanding therapist, who can help you identify and express your anger more effectively and enhance mutual understanding.

Excitement and Joy

Even your ecstatic feelings of new love are often hard to manage, especially within the context of marriage. You may find the manic quality of these emotions causes you to behave in adolescent ways. Are you waiting endlessly for phone calls or email engaging in risky behavior? Have you been ignoring y responsibilities? Perhaps you are unable to concentrate and you find yourself focused on the next sexual rendezvous. You may feel alive like never before. As wonderful as these feelings are, they often seem out of control.

There is an end point to such intense feelings. While you are going through them, it helps to remind yourself that they are normal. Just as the craziness of adolescence reaches completion, this tumult will also subside. You eventually need to set some parameters that will bring the focus back to yourself. When excitement rules, you think constantly and even obsess about your new attractions. Fear often intensifies after the initial bliss has receded. When that happens, you may become more motivated to search for peace by setting more limits on your behavior, becoming less impulsive, and developing a plan.

Rediscover Yourself

When you are feeling pressured to make everyone else happy, you will have difficulty recognizing your own needs and desires. If you have a girlfriend, even if the relationship is primarily in your mind, your attention will be given to her and to your husband as you attempt to balance two relationships. This requires tremendous effort. Your attention is on others and not on yourself. Your energy is sapped. Gradually you may begin to forget the things that brought you pleasure before you began to question your sexuality.

Your strategies for handling difficult situations were developed from lessons learned growing up in your family, your school, and your religious institutions. If your family encouraged free expression of feelings, you may address your struggles head on. However, most of us come from families with problems: addictions, abuse, mental illness, or overly rigid or lax rules and limits. When independent thinking and direct emotional expression are not permitted, we learn to hide our real self and develop ways to avoid our feelings, or to disguise them from others.

> *I've come to realize that I'm a lesbian who has been fighting it for twenty-two years. I'm married to a man who I've always thought I'd grow old with. But something is missing. I don't have the emotional-spiritual-sexual fulfillment I need to be whole. So I'm kicking and screaming inside, and I get stress-related diseases and overeat.*
>
> — SALLY

If you hold your feelings inside, like Sally does, you may find them expressed in physical ailments. Once you become aware of your emotions, no matter how painful, you will have access to your life force. You will know that every part of you is alive. If your feelings are alive, you will have more energy to face the issues that you could not face at earlier times. You may need to learn for the first time how to cope with all of these feelings. Yet it is a healthy instinct that urges you to remove your masks to find the hidden parts of you that need expression.

Do you feel that your happiness depends on the outcome of a new relationship? I remember feeling that my opportunity for passionate love was gone forever when my girlfriend left me. Eventually I discovered that my capacity to love didn't leave with her. I had discovered a love that was located inside my being. In the throes of a passionate love affair, it is hard to believe that anyone else could make you feel so deeply. You will feel more hopeful if you take ownership. The passion is a part of you. It is important to set aside time to evaluate your thoughts and pay attention to your emotions. This is a ripe time to learn about yourself. How can you find your way back to you? One woman writes about how she rediscovered herself:

> At first I tried yoga, and going to church, and that wasn't me. For the longest time, I would be without anything to think about or do without her near me. I planted a garden last spring, but it took me a year to do something alone that made me happy. I started reading again, I visited friends, I reconnected with my family. And within the last month, I have found that by doing all of those things, that like a bolt of lightning, I feel confident that I know myself. It's still hard. It's hard to hurt other people, it's hard not to be a pleaser, it's hard to face change and take risks. But I am confident that I'm not losing my mind, and it was "finding" myself that has secured that idea.
>
> — CLAUDIA

Claudia tried a range of activities that helped her to define herself. Some attempts were more useful than others. Think about how you might find undisturbed time for yourself. Do you schedule time to read, write, or take long walks? Have you given up your private time? Of course, daily life impinges on these opportunities, but if you set private time as a priority, it becomes part of your routine. Solitary times can be painful when you are in the midst of internal conflict. Unfortunately, it seems that suffering is usually required for personal growth.

Before you begin internal work, prepare yourself to manage the feelings that you will encounter. In fact, I believe this work is so challenging that it may be best to tackle with professional guidance. The first step is to clarify your methods for handling pain. Everyone has unhealthy habits or coping methods learned in childhood. You

ır eat excessively to push down feelings. You may sleep
......u or over-exercise. If you had a traumatic childhood, you
may have developed some self-destructive patterns, such as using
drugs, abusing alcohol, or engaging in compulsive spending or sexual activity. Try to be fearlessly honest with yourself when you make
a list of the unhealthy ways in which you handle or avoid difficult
feelings. The more conscious you are ahead of time, the less likely
you will be to resort to the old negative patterns that are best left
behind.

When You Feel Overwhelmed

The key to managing your crises during this journey is to be prepared. During your most lucid and least panicky moments, develop
a list of ways to help yourself during your darkest times. It is hard to
problem-solve or think rationally when you are overwhelmed. On
my message board, women offer their thoughts, taken from their
personal experiences, about how they have managed. Below is a
list of their ideas.

- *Surround yourself with things (yep, material) that reflect who you
  have been, are, and who you are becoming.*
- *Exercise: Walk the dog. Run. Practice yoga. Work out (whatever
  physical movement you enjoy).*
- *Journal: Write your thoughts and feelings just for yourself. This is
  particularly helpful when there's no one available to talk to.*
- *Read: For inspiration, information, or as a healthy escape.*
- *Find other women to talk to about your situation–it can be a life-
  saver.*

- *Talk openly with a family member. If you haven't already done this, consider whom you would feel safest with.*
- *Remind yourself that there are no sure things. If your relationship with your girlfriend ends, all you have left is you. So you'd better love yourself most.*
- *Make a list of your priorities, things you want to do, etc., and put them on a schedule. The more time you give yourself and the things that make you feel like you, the clearer you will become. For example:*

  o Dancing
  o Spending time with the kids
  o Visiting with parents and other relatives
  o Taking steps to find employment
  o Volunteering

You cannot drop out. It is not a solution to your problems. If you sleep all day, your problems will be waiting for you no matter how long you hide from them. Take baby steps toward gaining control of your life. The mindless routine things are the first steps. Take care of yourself. Basics. Eat, exercise, sleep. It doesn't have to be all in one day. Just baby steps . . . if you keep moving forward, you will eventually HAVE to get where you are meant to go.

— ANTOINETTE

Antoinette's advice is directed to a woman who is extremely depressed. Sadness and grief are a normal part of this transition. If you are not sleeping, or fatigued most of the time, experiencing extreme weight loss, having trouble focusing, or have lost interest or pleasure in almost all of your activities, you may be clinically depressed. Such depression requires professional treatment. Don't try to go through this alone; a therapist can offer you the needed support.

WHAT YOU CAN DO NOW

Remind yourself: Open yourself to your feelings, learn to manage them appropriately, and they will lead you to a satisfying experience. The roller coaster always comes to a stop eventually.

Ask yourself this question: What am I doing to take care of myself through the course of my ride?

Practice this technique for handling your emotions: Make a list of every healthy coping technique you have used or want to use when you are feeling overwhelmed or in pain. Keep the list easily accessible for your reference during your difficult times.

Take one step: Make a list of the things that brought you pleasure before you stepped onto your roller coaster. Choose one item from your list and reintroduce it into your life.

CHAPTER 6

GIRLFRIENDS: THE WOMEN YOU LOVE

Two years ago I fell in love with a woman; I was also physically attracted to her. The relationship never amounted to anything because she didn't return my feelings. But it got me thinking about the significance of my intense emotions. I wanted desperately to have a lesbian experience and since then I have. I would NEVER have had an affair with another man. I need to figure this out. What am I?

—VERONICA

For most married women, part of the process of exploring sexual identity is having a sexual experience. It is one thing to recognize your attraction to women, and yet another to know what sex is like with a woman. While your sexual identity is far more complex than whom you prefer to have sex with, it is still an important part of defining your sexuality.

A first relationship with another woman holds a special place in most women's lives. There is no way to view the relationship objectively, because it becomes a life marker. It often is a woman's first, perhaps only, experience of intimate love and of fulfilling sexual involvement. When anyone falls in love, there is a tendency to put that person on a pedestal. If the woman on the pedestal is a catalyst for dramatic life changes, she assumes even greater importance.

I maintained a friendship over many years with my first lover. Our intimate relationship came to an end gradually and painfully over the course of the year that I was making decisions about my marriage and my future lifestyle. I now know I probably would never have chosen to live my life with her. In many ways she was my teacher. With her, I learned about love, my sexual identity, and becoming more open and authentic.

We had a relationship dynamic that often occurs when the married woman's girlfriend has been out of the closet for many years. The teacher can get tired of her position and the married woman needs time to catch up to equalize the relationship. I felt that I couldn't ask for much from my friend. When she decided to leave town for another woman, I didn't ask her to stay. I knew that my marriage often left her waiting for my availability and I could make no promises about the future.

I, like many married women, needed to learn about the lesbian community. I couldn't generalize about relationships with women based on my first lover. In addition, I knew when I eventually left my husband that I was not ready or eager to get into another marital-type commitment immediately. My husband and I had known and dated each other for twenty years by the time we separated. I needed space to disentangle the knots and to handle the often-unpleasant negotiations and arguments related to divorce. Clearing away baggage helps set the groundwork for any new relationship. My girlfriend had been single for several years and wanted a fully committed relationship.

There are particular problems that can occur when a relationship develops while a woman is still married. It becomes difficult to assess the strength and viability of your marriage; the excitement and novelty of an affair can't compare to the mundane routines and responsibilities of marriage. Due to the increased volatility associated with an affair, most women have trouble staying focused on the larger picture in order to make appropriate decisions. If your affair survives a marital dissolution, you may continue to feel the situational stress for quite some time. In the following message, Dina speaks of a longing for the calmness of her marriage:

> We divorced a little over a year ago, and I have since struggled with all the issues associated with coming out. I have lived with my girlfriend for the past year, and our relationship has been very intense emotionally— with lots of highs and even more lows— something that I did not experience with my husband. I know I am gay, but the thought of raising my daughter in a loving, supportive, nonvolatile environment with both her parents sounds like the way to go to me right now. Am I crazy for going back to a life that I was so eager to leave?
>
> — DINA

While you are still searching for your direction, the significant people in your life are often reacting to you. When you react, little is accomplished. In the face of other people's hurt or anger, it is often difficult to remain focused on yourself.

Dina is noticing a relationship dynamic that is different between two women versus a man and a woman. The intensity between women is usually greater. From childhood, females are trained to be more expressive and aware of emotions than men. These traits, of course, are gender stereotypes, but they tend to be true in many cases. Emotional expressiveness and deep connection may be what attracts you to another woman. Yet, it may be the first time you've had to handle a partner's feelings, or even your own. Increased passion appears not just sexually, but in all areas of the relationship. You may feel angrier, more jealous, or more excited than you have before. The steadiness and rationality of the marriage may suddenly look inviting. While there are similarities in any relationship, there are some differences between heterosexual and lesbian relationships. Each comes with its own set of challenges.

I spent so long trying to decide what I should do based on how my husband and then my girlfriend would react. I totally lost myself in their needs.

— GAIL

If, like Gail, you have lost your bearings, it may help to schedule more time alone to examine your feelings free of outside influences. Some women decide to take a break from their girlfriend for that reason. Anything that helps you to be less distracted by the stresses of the affair will help to redirect your attention to larger decisions that need to be made. You must understand the role of the extramarital relationship in your life. Is it an isolated affair or a catalyst for examining your sexual orientation?

An affair usually disrupts your marriage, even when it's kept secret. If it leads to hard work on the marriage, you can begin to look at the underlying causes of unrest that led to the affair. When you take the time to learn from the affair and recover from related wounds, your marriage may become even stronger in the aftermath. However, sometimes a marital assessment leads to the conclusion that the problems are irreconcilable. If the issues that led to infidelity involve sexual identity, they are more difficult to resolve.

Your unhappiness with your husband may simply be that he is a man, and not a woman.

Should I Reveal My Attraction to Her?

I want to tell my close friend/coworker that I have fallen madly in love with her, but don't want to ruin our friendship. We connect on every level and talk about everything. I'm afraid that she doesn't feel the same way about me, or she doesn't want to admit that she does. Should I take the chance and tell her how I feel, or stay silent?

— JAYNE

When you are considering whether to tell a friend about your feelings for her, you need to consider the possible ramifications. She may feel the same or differently. The revelation can lead you to an affair or to awkwardness in the friendship. It could possibly lead to losing a friend, a job, or your marriage. If you don't want to shake up your world, try to create some distance from your friend until your emotions diminish. However, if you are unable to let go of your feelings, you may need to take some risks. A direct talk may be your best course of action if you continue to feel internal pressures to pursue this romance. If you do, make sure you have a support system in place to help you handle any outcome.

I am in love with a woman who has no clue, but I cannot say anything. I fear the rejection and humiliation that may arise if she doesn't feel the same. Seeing her every day is torture. Why does this kind of love have to hurt so much? Why is it so wrong?

—NOREEN

This woman and I flirt a lot. I know I do not do this with just any friend. We spend a lot of time together, and I am going to burst if I don't say anything about the way I feel. It's just a huge step and a huge let-down and embarrassment if she isn't interested. I'm so lost and confused.

— DOLLY

When you have strong feelings as Dolly and Noreen do, the stakes are high. You may want reassurance that your friend feels the same as you before you take any action. But no one, except she, can give you that. A straight woman may flirt and act playful, especially if that is the way you are relating to her. When I first became conscious of my feelings for women, I would sometimes read things into other women's behavior. I could have sworn that a woman I played racquetball with was incredibly flirtatious with me; and I had so much fun with it. Yet she was happily married. When you have such strong feelings for a friend, it may be time to learn about the meaning of your attraction. If you decide to take a risk, there are ways of letting your friend know that you are questioning your sexuality without saying she is the reason. The information may give her an opportunity to let you know if she feels the same way.

Four years ago, I fell in love with a woman, but since she was straight like me, we classified our relationship as soul mates. I really did love her and told her so. I got turned on whenever we were close or had any physical contact, but I never told her that part. That relationship never amounted to anything because she didn't return my feelings, and I don't have contact with her anymore.

— JO

Jo's decision to keep her emotions to herself probably simplified her life. Her attraction was significant enough to move her into further exploration. Yet she remained clear that the subsequent questions that were raised were not related specifically to her friend, but to herself. In contrast, Monica decided to be direct with her friend, and the doors opened to new possibilities.

I can remember sitting in front of a campfire, with this beautiful "out" lesbian sitting across from me. We locked eyes . . . and held them for quite some time, and for the first time, I didn't look away. And I knew that she knew . . . she knew how I felt, I was beginning to open myself, and let out the butterfly! About an hour later, we left on a midnight canoe ride that forever changed my life. Reaching for a beverage, I rocked the canoe. I let out a sigh, and said, "Do ya wanna rock the boat"? A loon rose beside the boat, and let out a long beautiful echo across the lake. You could have heard a pin drop. The stars twinkled above us, and I knew my life had changed in an instant!!! Today? My girlfriend and I own a house, and are raising my children together.

— MONICA

Not every woman's attempt at direct communication has as happy an ending as Monica's story. But the chances of fulfilling your fantasy are at least possible when you speak the truth. One woman described an experience that was very upsetting to her:

I became quite friendly with a co-worker who I was convinced was gay. I let her know that although I'm still married, I am a lesbian. She increased her contact with me and we became even closer. I felt that we'd gotten close enough to ask if she was

*involved with anyone. She freaked out and asked if I was mak-
ing a pass and told me that I had crossed the personal issues
line. Furthermore, she told me she was straight.*

— MARISOL

In contrast, when I realized I was attracted to my friend, I sensed
that I would not face rejection. I never anticipated that telling her
about my feelings would turn my world around. Once I became
involved with her, the questions I had about my sexuality were completely about her. Did I want to be with her or with my husband?
Only after she left town and she was no longer available was I able
to look more directly at myself.

Computer Love

The internet can offer previously unknown support to many
women who are terribly isolated, but online communication also has
its perils. Some women fall in love, having spent little or no face-to-
face time with their romantic partner. The real life relationship often
seems very different from what was envisioned, and at times disap-
pointing. Written communication leaves a lot of room for fantasy
and subjective interpretation. Many people find it easier to be open
and vulnerable in communication online; there is a built-in distance
that sometimes provides a feeling of safety. Phone contact offers
more information, but it still doesn't reveal the nuances of your girlfriend's living habits, how she interacts with other people, and many
other things that you only learn by being with a person over time.

Nan told me about falling in love with a woman whom she met
in a chat room. "We spend hours together each day, online and on
the phone," Nan told me. The intimacy created by the frequency

and intensity of contact over the internet may be different in real time. Anonymity and the sense of safety of online correspondence often encourage a more rapid exposure of intimate details about your thoughts and feelings. Yet if you live in different parts of the country or world, it is hard to find ways to get to know each other in person and experience each other in daily living. Long-distance relationships in general have many difficulties. There is a greater chance of forming a lasting union if you choose to pursue a woman who lives close enough to take the relationship offline. If you meet a woman online, try to get to know her in real time as soon as possible so that you can evaluate the relationship with greater clarity.

> *I am losing faith in ever finding a sane woman to love. I have met several women online who were open and warm, with many shared interests. When we arranged to meet (after traveling a long distance), they were not at all the way they had presented themselves. I have been hurt terribly by being physically rejected by one woman and emotionally brutalized by another. Several women said they had no problems with my plans to continue living with my husband, but after a few months, they were angry and rejecting.*
>
> *— ERIN*

You can't judge a woman by words alone. It takes live time to feel the interactions that comprise relationships. Words online are often shared desires, interests, and goals. While these are important points of confluence and joining when you get to know someone, they are just one part of the picture. Words over the internet will not communicate body language or the ability to express warmth in person. There are whole constellations of sensual interactions that occur between human beings when they are attempting to form intimate relations. Computer communication can never give us this information. Theoretically, people often believe they will be fine with a situation such as Erin's arrangement with her husband. But they don't know for certain until they actually try it out.

Can a New Relationship Survive?

Is there anyone out there who knows of a happy ending to all of this? It seems that all this strife and anguish just leads us to more strife and anguish. Can two women, who have been married and had children, fall in love and live happily ever after?

— KASI

While it is difficult to begin a relationship in the midst of turmoil, that doesn't mean it can't survive; it is just more challenging. You may long for, but cannot rely on, a happy ending to a relationship that you are just forming. Most women who make their way through the difficult process of redefining their marriage and facing the hurdles of coming out to themselves eventually find a happier life. The entire journey requires so much self-examination that your enrichment is a by-product of traveling this path. You may be disappointed if you set the goal of "ever after" with your new love. Try to leave that to fate. Keep working on the current issues at hand and keep your communication open with your partner. If you have felt a new level of intensity in this relationship, recognize the experience as a blessing. No one can predict whether this new relationship will last. However, you now know a depth of feeling that is a part of you, and the memory is permanent. It may become a new reference point for this or any future intimate relationship.

I left husband, home, and children nine months ago. After the initial euphoria feeling of HIGH as a KITE, along came Christmas and the worst depression of my life. I'm worried sick about money, missing all that's familiar, guilty as hell. My new girlfriend moved into my flat . . . it has been so painful. I can't deal with it all and promise her a future. I feel I can't go back, or forward, in fact, I have seriously wondered if life will ever be tolerable again.

— MAYA

Both you and your girlfriend should be prepared for the indecision and vacillation that are so common for married women. The decision-making process involves trial and error, which occurs while the relationship is still an affair, and often continues after marital separation. It takes time to grieve many losses before moving into another union. As evidenced by Maya's message, if the grieving doesn't occur before you make your decisions, it is likely to take place later and will impact your new relationship. This doesn't mean that you and your girlfriend cannot progress toward commitment, but you will need to survive many twists and turns along the way. This is a complicated way to start a new relationship.

I have been with a woman whom I am deeply in love with for about two-and-a-half years now. I find that as I try to redefine myself and my lifestyle, I keep pushing her away. It's almost as if she is smothering me. I am still very much in love with her, but I can't be with her all the time anymore.

— RACHEL

Both Maya and Rachel are facing the difficulties of moving directly from marriage into a new relationship. Timing is often the key to the survival of any relationship, no matter how much two people love each other. In the case of two women, timing is related to how long each of you has known you are gay and whether you have reached some resolution in prior committed relationships. The degree to which you have completed these tasks will affect how ready you are to build a new, long-term commitment.

If the woman in your life is clear about her sexual identity, is single, and is prepared for a commitment, her needs are different from yours. She will want time with you to share important events and to integrate you into her daily life. These desires would be reasonable if you were more available. You are still making decisions about extricating yourself from the marital commitment and moving into a new lifestyle. Even after making the decision to leave, you may want to take some time to experience your independence. Some women decide to live alone while they adjust to their new situation. The difference in competing needs can sometimes lead to conflict.

> *My girlfriend struggles with the fact that I am still in my marriage. No matter how I try to ease her mind, she is tortured by the thought of my husband touching me. I am slowly working my way out, but she doesn't seem to see any movement. I have explained that a lot of my movement is emotional and cannot be seen externally. While she does understand that, she remains in a confused and tortured state.*
>
> — CARMEN

Like Carmen, you may have difficulty convincing your lover that you are making changes. The experience of waiting often feels interminable for your partner. Nevertheless, there are no shortcuts on this journey. You must give yourself as much time as you need to work on yourself and your situation. You cannot fit yourself into your girlfriend's timetable. Nor can she do that for you. Each of you needs to attend to your own set of tasks.

You may believe you are communicating the intention of building a future with your girlfriend. She often sees it differently. If you are moving slower than she expected, she may view your sincere intentions as empty promises. A married woman named Esther writes about this conflict in her message:

The woman who I fell in love with, and who fell in love with me, is distancing herself because I am married and she is in pain. She knows that at this time, breaking up my family isn't possible. I do intend to leave, yet I simply am not ready.

— ESTHER

Despite Esther's intentions, neither she nor her partner can know for certain that she will leave her marriage. You may feel that you love your partner deeply, but you are still married. Until you are ready to leave or change your marital structure, you have obstacles to overcome. You cannot make effective decisions based on what you wish for or fear about the future. Your decisions must be based on what is happening in the present. A wise Buddhist woman captured the futility of grasping too tightly to any relationship:

"You need to come face to face with a truth about yourself. There is a big empty place you're trying to fill up with this (woman). You're clutching to this relationship to feel secure, but security comes from completely letting go of all control and allowing yourself to feel whatever you fear. You are trying to create solid ground under your feet so you don't have to experience being

alone, but if you would let go, you'd find that the emptiness you fear is really a still and restful place."

— CHARLOTTE KASL, PH.D.

IF THE BUDDHA DATED

Eventually you will know whether the relationship will last, but this cannot be your primary goal. The changes you must make reach beyond the outcome of any single relationship. Rhea's message, filled with regrets, illustrates this point:

I left my marriage when I had an affair with a woman. Then she left me. I am completely alone for the first time in my life and finding it hard to cope. It is hard to meet suitable women, and I feel so sad about what I've done to the family. I'm not at all sure now about my decision to leave my husband, though I was at the time.

— RHEA

You face new levels of grief if your extramarital relationship ends, but you may eventually find solace in discovering new meaning to that relationship. If this is your first intimate relationship with a woman, she may be the catalyst for your coming-out process. Anna finds comfort in viewing her girlfriend that way:

My "catalyst girlfriend" had a change of heart, and so I stand naked and alone. At the same time, though, it is where I need to be in order to move forward, wherever forward is!"

— ANNA

How You Can Help the New Relationship

There are some things you can do to strengthen a new relationship. Try to keep your communication with your girlfriend honest, even when you make a decision she doesn't like. New romances can appear to be problem free, especially when you two talk easily about the problems with your husband. However, differences and struggles will eventually appear in any relationship. When areas of conflict do arise, now is the time to set the groundwork for good communication. Address your conflicts directly. Remember the importance of being true to yourself, while remaining sensitive to your partner.

We all have a part in creating relationship difficulties. Take time to explore how you contributed to the marital problems. You have an opportunity now to handle yourself differently with your girlfriend. Whether or not the relationship survives, you will benefit from making necessary changes in your relationship patterns.

A Note to Girlfriends

At the start of your relationship, you confronted a dilemma as difficult as that which your married partner faced. If her marriage was conventional, she had to decide whether to break the bonds of commitment. When you fell in love, you had to decide whether to get involved with someone married and with limited availability. Both of you chose to cross a line that promised complications. When your heart is on fire, your decisions are not usually pragmatic.

The relationship, started as an extramarital involvement, had a chaotic beginning. Finding a more peaceful way to be together will take time, possibly years. Your married lover may look for some structure from you. She needs you to let her know when you have reached your limits, even if she may not like it. In the following message, for example, Paige writes her girlfriend about the emotional upheaval that keeps her paralyzed.

When I am with my husband, I feel guilty that I am not with you. And when I am with you, I feel guilty that I am not with my husband. I am doing the best I can and don't have any more to give at this point in time. It is up to you to decide whether that is enough for now.

— PAIGE

It's hard to say "no" or "enough" when you are afraid of losing your partner. However, it helps her to know that you are taking responsibility for yourself. She doesn't have to second-guess how you are feeling. You must always evaluate how long you are willing to wait. It takes courage to be in your position; many women can't tolerate that insecurity. I hear from many married women whose lovers left town or found another partner before they could come to a decision. Is it time to stop putting your life on hold? This is the primary dilemma confronting you. How long is too long?

I know that in falling in love with a married woman, I was setting myself up for heartbreak. But I'm here now, and my feelings have given me no reprieve. I wonder if instead of her making a decision, she is just waiting to see who will tire of this first. Me or her husband?

— RHONA

Rhona expresses feelings that each person in the love triangle feels at different times. It is not unusual for people to stay in limbo for months, even years, rather than make a painful decision. When the pain outweighs the pleasure, you will know that it is time to do something different. What can you do, as the other woman, to help yourself and the relationship?

While you are still committed to her, avoid destroying the positive feelings that you have. Marylou is struggling with this:

> *I've been involved with my girlfriend for a year. At first she was all excited about leaving her marriage. She tried one time, but he threatened her. So she didn't leave. I worry every day about whether she sleeps with him or not. She says he offers her nothing, but she has to rely on him for health care benefits. She stopped saying she will leave. I think of calling it quits. She says she loves me but isn't doing anything to be with me. I think she has recently started lying to me. I don't know what to do anymore.*
>
> — MARYLOU

If you feel threatened or scared that your lover will never leave her husband, you may react by clutching tighter. But when you do, you are often creating the very situation that you are trying to avoid. If she feels smothered or pressured, you may find you are pushing her away. Try to give her space to make her decisions.

Use the same advice I gave to your married partner. Get the focus back on yourself. A life of waiting will eventually undermine your self-confidence and vitality. Find ways to enjoy yourself that are independent of your girlfriend. If you must wait for a time, use your time wisely learn how to make yourself happy. Recall what you did for enjoyment prior to meeting your married girlfriend that you may have let go.

Therapy can be helpful at this time, not only for support, but to examine how you got yourself into this situation. There may be some hidden benefits to being involved with a married woman. If you are not ready for a commitment, if you too are recovering form another relationship, you may feel safe with the natural limits of this involvement. It looks as if the married woman sets all of the relationship boundaries, but when she becomes available, you may feel the pressure of her new availability. It is important, therefore, to resolve your unfinished business regarding intimacy and commitment. Any way you come to understand yourself better will come to benefit your future, with or without your girlfriend.

WHAT YOU CAN DO NOW

Remind yourself: It's better to speak up for yourself and face your girlfriend's anger than to live in fear or sacrifice your integrity.

Ask yourself this question: Am I making decisions that I can accept regardless of the outcome of my new relationship?

Practice this technique for handling your feelings: When you are anxious about whether your relationship can survive the many challenges, do the following exercise:

- List all the reasons you want this relationship to continue.
- List all the possible advantages to this relationship ending. (This may be difficult, but take your time and stay with it).
- What are some steps you can take toward becoming more secure in yourself?

Take one step: Carve out a time in the day just for yourself (even as brief as ten to fifteen minutes), with no interruptions, to write, think, or meditate. Begin the practice of focusing inward to learn about your needs and desires.

CHAPTER 7

HELPING YOUR CHILDREN

Some Common Questions Related to Your Children's Well-Being

How Will My Kids Be Affected?

At every stage of your sexual awakening, your children are affected. If you doubt this, you need only look at the reactions and intuition your children have shown regarding smaller events in their lives. If you are depressed, happy, or emotionally volatile, they pick up your cues, they know something is up, they speak with concern or unexpected wisdom when you least expect it.

Your ability to parent may suffer because you are currently in crisis. You might feel guilty about your less-than-perfect mothering, which may sometimes even verge on neglectful. These slumps are very much a part of the parenting process throughout your life cycle. Anyone facing a potential life change, even possible divorce, is going to be more self-centered. When you feel guilty, it helps to remind yourself that an increased amount of focus on yourself is necessary in order to address the many questions that are at issue.

I am a married mom who leaves her kids every weekend to stay with my girlfriend, and I feel GUILTY.

— SARA

I feel I might be doing harm to the kids that could be saved if I would really try to work things out with my husband.

— MARIE

Like many women, you may have begun this exploration in response to an attraction to another woman, so your attention may be inordinately focused on her. If this behavior is out of character for you, it can create confusion and internal conflict, which, in turn, requires even more self-involvement. If you think your kids don't know anything is different just because you haven't told them, you are probably wrong.

Children notice the changes in your availability if you are involved physically or emotionally in a love affair. After all, you are going through the emotional volatility of questioning your sexuality, your values, your marriage, and the very essence of who you thought you were and are. Your children may not understand what is happening, but they usually will know that something is different and often upsetting to the family status. If they seem worried about you or your husband, you should address their concerns. How you talk to them will depend on their developmental level. For instance, younger children need confirmation that you have been upset lately, along with your reassurance that you will continue to care for their needs. They also need to hear that your unhappiness or family strife is not their fault. You can be more specific with an older child, who will understand, without hearing details, that you are having a hard time, feeling depressed, etc., and that you are working to resolve the problems.

It was a hard time for both my kids and me when I became involved with a woman while married. I stayed away from home far more often than I had previously. When I was home with them, I was often distracted. I recall some advice I received at the time from a therapist: "I should try harder to enjoy my kids. I could have fun with them, rather than seeing parenting as a chore." At the time, the advice felt terrible to me. I felt incapable of enjoying my kids—I had too much going on in my internal world. The only way I could think of myself was selfish. If you don't have the advantage of hindsight, you may struggle with similar feelings. This type of self-centered behavior, I discovered, disappears when you begin to find some answers.

Guilt, although common, is not helpful for most married women with children, and you need to work actively to confront your feelings of self-condemnation. You would never have chosen to put your kids through this difficulty. It's hard to see them suffer at all. However, children generally do survive—they can be quite resilient if both spouses have their best interest in mind. It is next to impossible to be a good parent when you are going through emotional turmoil. You can only do the best you can while you are going through it. At the same time, I know of no way to find answers to these important questions without delving into the issues.

Keisha, a client of mine, was obsessed with the excitement of her first sexual involvement with a woman and spent as much time as possible with her girlfriend in the beginning of their relationship. People in Keisha's life began to notice and remarked on her absence from home. Despite her feelings of guilt, Keisha continued to act out of character. She lied to people concerning her whereabouts and overlooked many of her regular responsibilities. She felt like an adolescent in the throes of sexual discovery.

You too may feel like you hardly know yourself. Despite your guilty feelings, you may be avoiding your parenting responsibilities. When your life becomes more even and you feel more at peace and clear about your direction, you will likely have the energy to refocus on the kids. At that time, you may need to devote extra care and attention to them. One way to reframe your guilt is to see it as a reflection of your concern. Try not to beat yourself up. Parenting is a lifelong process, and once you get through this stage of your life, you can take lots of time working to be the best parent you can be. Keisha felt so much happier once she found her way to the other side of the questioning maze. She brought that happiness into her parenting. She wrote:

I am a better mom since acknowledging myself (in a thousand different ways). Not sick, depressed, unmotivated, controlling, or sheepish anymore. This is MY life, too. My children are happy, thriving, and loved.

— KEISHA

Should I Stay Married for the Kids?

Once you move through the blissful stage of first discovery, you must turn to the reality that decisions need to be made. Even if you decide that you want to separate from your husband in order to reach better self-understanding, you may feel confounded by concern for your children. One of the most painful decisions to address is whether to stay in the marriage for the sake of the kids.

My girlfriend of three years recently broke up with me because she was tired of living like we had an affair. Whenever I left the kids, I felt terribly guilty and eventually spent less and less time with her. I feel bad now and miss her terribly. I have set a goal to stay with my husband for five more years until both teens have graduated from high school. Is a goal like this logical?

— BETSY

To answer Betsy's question for yourself, it may help to understand what is informing your decision. Then, you must decide for yourself whether it is realistic to maintain a marriage just for the sake of the kids. This decision should take into account what kind of problems preexisted this particular time of questioning. Are there problems that you still have hopes of correcting? Have the problems been hurting your children?

You, like the rest of the society, are influenced by our culture, which often tells us that children will be damaged by divorce. There is research that supports both sides of the discussion—that most kids will be irreparably harmed, or that they will be resilient and ultimately fare well. Many factors influence the eventual well-being of the children. If you face an extremely contentious divorce, if your husband is homophobic, or if you have had problems parenting as a marital team, your children are likely to suffer more. If you and your husband have a history of cooperative parenting and a desire to focus on the children's welfare above all else, your kids will survive a divorce far better.

If you decide to divorce, you will need to consider your timing. Sometimes it is hard to wait another minute once you have made your decision. You need to balance your desire to start moving on with the events and challenges facing your kids and your husband. After Keisha became certain she was a lesbian, she decided that she wanted to divorce. However, she also wanted to be as responsible as she could for her children. She decided to wait another year, until her oldest son graduated from high school. In fact, that time permitted her to come out to the people she needed to before she moved. When her son, Mark, graduated, she decided she needed to wait until after his birthday.

If you, like Keisha, notice that new obstacles keep appearing in your projected plan, you need to reexamine your fears. You may have more work to do regarding your comfort level about your move. Do you keep finding another marker that postpones your decision, like a birthday or vacation or your child's graduation? Remember, there is no perfect time to break up your family. After a few more delays, and realizing that she needed to face her fears about starting over, Keisha made the move.

If you feel terribly depressed about your marriage, you may question the wisdom of staying with your husband at the expense of your happiness and mental health. Jean struggled with her unhappiness for three years before she finally decided to separate from her husband. In the following message, she shared an important insight:

I strongly believe that, if possible, children should be raised by both parents—whatever type of family it may be. But if that's not possible, then why not give them the next best thing— a happy mother? I was unhappy, unhealthy, and not a good mom. Now I am happy, much healthier, and working on that every day, and a MUCH better mom. My children deserve that. I choose to live close to my ex-husband so that he can have as much access to the children as he wants. I want to work together with him in that way. And because he is a better dad, now that he has to concentrate on it and make it a priority when he has them, our kids are thriving.

—JEAN

If you decide to let go of an affair in your effort to recommit to your marriage, you will go through a period of grieving. During this time, your kids may be worried about you. As your grief subsides at a gradual pace, they will generally move on to focusing on themselves and their own developmental tasks.

Should I Tell the Kids?

If you are age-appropriately open with your children about the changes you are making, you will encourage more openness from them. There are a few specific situations involving the kids that require extra caution, which I will discuss later. Openness is important, but on your own timetable. It is best to wait until you know what direction you are taking, both regarding your marriage and your sexuality. If you are planning to separate or change the structure of your family, focus on that transition will usually take priority over discussion about your sexuality. However, every situation is unique, and what needs to be discussed often depends on how much the kids have witnessed directly.

It may help to work on your own attitude and beliefs about divorce and sexuality before talking to your children. You will offer them more comfort if you are sincerely optimistic about handling the upcoming changes and are comfortable enough about your sexuality to communicate self-acceptance. When you are ready to talk about your sexuality, remember that your children see you as their role model. If you feel shame or hide a relationship that becomes obvious to them, you are sending a message. Silence or dishonesty can suggest that the issue is too embarrassing to address. Take as much time as you need to be sure you give your kids a positive view of lesbianism. This will make their ultimate acceptance much easier. Remember, though, that it may take your children time to adapt to your changes and become fully comfortable with your sexuality.

How much time this will take depends on their ages and their prior attitudes about homosexuality. Older children may have been influenced by a homophobic environment for a longer time than kids in early elementary school or younger. However, there are many more schools and communities that communicate acceptance of gay and lesbian youth today than when I came out in the '70s. Gay parents are often not as hidden. Nevertheless, homophobia still exists in many places. If you or your husband or members of your family have openly expressed homophobic attitudes in the past, your kids will have to work harder to overcome those values. Like you, they have to undo previous prejudices and fears about gay people. Under the best of circumstances, it takes about two years for a complete, comfortable acceptance. The argument for openness is different with children if your ultimate decision is to maintain your marriage.

In this case, you should question your reason for coming out to a child at this time and under these circumstances. Honesty is important, but if there is no pressing reason for your child to know about your sexuality, it's usually best to avoid getting into it while you still live with your husband. You can help your child by demonstrating a general acceptance of different lifestyles and ranges of sexuality. To start this discussion while you're still married, and planning to be for the foreseeable future, usually requires your child to hold on to a deep family secret. Such a discussion may raise even more questions: How do you know you are a lesbian? Are you involved with someone? Why are you still with Dad? etc... Your children do not need to know about your sex life or your desires.

Another exception to disclosing your sexuality relates to custody concerns. If you have good reason to believe that your husband or a family member will fight to have your children taken from you, you may need to hide your outside relationship from both your husband and your kids. Again, it is unfair to put your kids in the position of having to keep a secret from their father or other family members. It's usually best to keep everything to yourself and seek guidance from an attorney until all custody issues are settled.

When Is the Right Time?

You need to look at both your own and your children's readiness when considering the right time to talk to them. Children demand different approaches based on their level of maturity.

I think the biggest homophobia I have to deal with is in myself.
Are my kids going to be okay?

— LIN

If you hear yourself expressing inordinate fears about your children, if you think you're victimizing them, setting them up for a life of pain, and so on, take a step back and look into yourself. Like Lin, you must start with your own feelings of discomfort. How much of this concern is coming from your unresolved feelings about gay people and the gay lifestyle? Can you picture yourself in a happy, well-adjusted relationship with a woman? Are you able to envision some advantages your children might have growing up with a lesbian mom? Can you see a lesbian lifestyle as a healthy alternative? You may have to work hard to find loving self-acceptance before you have the discussion with your children. A gay-sensitive therapist or a coming-out support group can help you in this process.

When the time is right, you will be able to communicate that this new, same-sex attraction is just another form of loving, which should be honored and cherished just like any other loving relationship. Most of the homophobia that children will confront comes from ignorance or fear. If Lin's relationship continues to be a happy, affectionate, and loving one, her kids will learn through example that a lesbian relationship is as good as any other.

I've told all of my kids now except the one who is still in school and living at home. I was going to wait until she is out of school and doesn't have to deal with all of the petty stuff that can happen at a small school. But I'm afraid that if she ever finds out that I told the others two years before her, she'll be even more hurt and angry and feel even more deceived. The other kids have basically abandoned me completely at this point. They are clinging to the safety and security of their dad. I want to cling to the last one, who doesn't know about me and therefore doesn't know that she should shun me. Should I wait, or should I keep the train rolling?

— TASHA

Tasha's dilemma highlights the question of whether your silence is a response to protecting your kids or to protecting yourself from conflict. Sometimes older children will feel betrayed by being kept in the dark about your sexuality. For instance, Michael, a teenager who contacted me, had bitter words regarding his lesbian mother: "From the perspective of a son whose mother came out after being a closeted lesbian for many years, I can tell you that my anger comes from the lies." He added, "That doesn't mean she shouldn't have come out, but we can't all fall into line and be the perfect little family again." It would help Michael to hear from his mother that women who come out later in life often have a harder time coming to self-acceptance. Her dishonesty was probably a result of her fears. She could not tell him something that she wasn't prepared to tell his father or even possibly admit to herself. Michael's words may help you to understand how important it is to communicate patience and that there is certainly no guarantee of immediate acceptance. It may take your children some time to accept all that has occurred, but if you have had a good relationship up until now, it will help you all get through this.

What Should I Say?

When is a child old enough to hear about my sexuality?

— MIRA

A child is never too young or too old to learn about your sexuality. The factors that need to be considered are the timing of the disclosure, the reason for the disclosure, and the way it is communicated. If your child is facing some difficult transitions or is in crisis, it may be better to wait for a calmer time. If you believe the time is right to tell your child, he or she, at any age, can find a way to understand and incorporate this information. Of course, it is essential that your discussion be offered in an age-appropriate manner. There are professionals in the mental health field who will suggest differently, but most who have extensive experience with the issues will propose offering children a foundation of honesty from their earliest years.

Age and maturity level enter into the decision of how and what to tell your children. I came out to my kids after I separated and became immediately involved with my lover. The kids were young (seven and nine years old). I now realize that coming out to them came from my need—not theirs. I felt so excited, I just wanted the world to know. But the kids were only worried about our family—they had the usual fears that most children have about divorce. Would both of their parents still be a loving presence in their lives? They were not irreparably damaged by my premature revelation, but, in fact, they didn't need to know about my sexuality at that time.

If you have an infant or a toddler, you must maintain a semblance of calmness while in contact with your baby. A child up to three years old needs to develop a sense of security, a sense that you will continue taking care of his or her needs. It may require serious work to keep your anxiety separate from your child while you are on this difficult journey. At this age, your child has little understanding of time and mostly needs to feel some steadiness and reliability. You can offer this through your words and through maintaining a routine, whether with you or with a substitute caregiver.

Children from ages three to five, upon noticing your emotional changes and volatility, will often see themselves as the cause. They need verbal reassurances that they are not to blame. Hugs, kisses, and adherence to daily routine will help them. If you and your husband separate during this time, your children will primarily need reassurance. Above all, they need to know that they are not being abandoned.

If your child is in grammar school, listen carefully to reports of any behavioral problems on the playground or in the classroom. If you have been very unhappy or upset at home, your child may feel sad for you, may become distracted by worries or melancholy at school or begin acting out. At this stage, it is important to let your child know that you are paying attention and want to help her. If she is having problems, you need to be careful to avoid parenting out of guilt. If your child is acting angry, you can let her know that you feel concerned about her unhappiness, but she cannot behave in destructive, hurtful ways. You may be tempted to give in or feel sorry for her because you believe you caused this upheaval. Your child needs your help in creating behavioral control. Your attention in this way will help her in her developmental task of making friends in the school. (For more information see *What About the Kids?: Raising Your Children Before, During, and After Divorce*, by Judith S. Wallerstein and Sandra Blakeslee, in the References section.)

Usually young kids don't need to know about your sexuality unless you are in a committed relationship or they are seeing some new behaviors they do not understand. Try to pay attention to questions or expressions of confusion about the meaning of your new relationship. If I had given my children more time to observe my new way of life, they would eventually have wondered about my new love relationship. A relevant discussion at that point may have had more meaning to them than my assumption of their interest in our initial discussion.

If your children ask you direct questions about your sexuality, they are ready to know. Kids sometimes offer hints related to their curiosity about your sexuality. For instance, they may suddenly bring up issues about homosexuality more than usual. They may ask how you feel about someone being gay or ask you whether your friends are gay. It's generally best to answer their questions honestly. If you feel ready, this may be an opportunity to tell them about your sexuality. In most cases, it is inappropriate to tell them about your sexual preference before your husband knows, because that places them in the position of holding a secret from another family member.

Adolescence can be an especially complicated time to learn about a parent's homosexuality. Nina wrote to me about her thirteen-year-old son who has become "emotionally withdrawn since my divorce and has become silent like his father was. He used to be physically very affectionate and now seems to be going deeper and deeper into himself, refusing to share his feelings anymore."

I told Nina that her son was facing many tasks that all adolescents encounter. This is a time when children are focused on their own sexual development and exploration. They are usually self-centered for some of the same reasons that you may be at this time. You're working on redefining your identity, developing a new peer group, and exploring your sexuality again. Your adolescents' primary challenges are to develop a peer group, to experience their own physical/sexual changes, and to begin to experiment with their sexuality, eventually forming a sexual identity. You can imagine how difficult it would be for your teenager to witness you confronting similar issues. He wants you to be his rock, not to project the same confusion that he is experiencing. Your teenager may also worry more than kids of other ages about his friends' reactions; acceptance is a particularly high priority at this age.

You need to protect your adolescent from most of the details of your sex life. He or she is maturing, but is still a child and needs parental boundaries regarding your private life. Some teens may need special understanding when they try to keep friends at a distance or they appear angry. Remember, this is a natural time for kids to express their independence, often with angry, oppositional behavior. They want their independence, but they also want you to continue being their mother and protector. Although they may fight you, they need you to hold firm to your rules and limits.

It took me a long time to recognize that not all of my children's difficult phases were related to my sexual reorientation. You may experience a similar realization concerning your children's behavior as you watch for signs of dysfunction. Eventually you may even have some laughs when you discover that what you thought was a sign of some deep, troubling response to your life change was only about the fact that your kid's friends didn't invite him to the ball game.

How Do I Approach My Kids?

Although my five-year marriage is over and we started divorce proceedings last week, my husband has been very supportive of my new lifestyle. My sons, ages twenty-one, twenty-three, and twenty-four, are from my first marriage. Their father is deceased. My oldest son is independent and living six hundred miles away. However, he was recently engaged and is planning a fall wedding. My middle son is attending college close by and is home frequently. My youngest son has not found his way in life and is living part-time with us. How shall I reveal this to my sons, and should I do it alone or with my husband?

— ELIZABETH

The way to approach children tends to be highly individualized. If you are in a second marriage, whether your husband should be with you when you talk to the kids depends on how involved he has been with them. If he has a close relationship with them, it could be very helpful to have him available when you talk. If he is working with you, as in Elizabeth's case, it might help them to see his support of you and that there is no malice between you. However, if he has not been very involved with them, I suggest you talk to them by yourself. Your discussion may need to be ongoing with each. Rather than try to talk to all of the kids together, speak to them separately and give each time to react and to understand. Older children often need to hear something about your process of coming out. For example, Elizabeth found it helpful for her sons to know that she had questioned her sexuality for a long time but had never been able to face it directly until recently.

Like Elizabeth, you need to focus on honesty, but that does not mean you have to include all details. Welcome your children's questions and let them know that you love them and want them to be happy. You may tell them that this should not change their relationship with you. Try to be patient—allow them time to reach acceptance. If you have had a good relationship in the past, it should carry you through this. Above all, remember to trust in your children's desire to love you.

Should They Know About My Girlfriend?

How and when can I bring my partner into my children's lives? I have been involved with one woman for the past two years, and I am feeling more sure than I have ever felt about anyone that she is my life partner. Currently, because of my husband (we still live together) and the fact that he blames our upcoming divorce on her, she has not been physically integrated into my children's lives.

— GINNY

"I would wait until you two live apart," I told Ginny, "when your husband won't have to directly observe your changing lifestyle. There usually is no rush for the children to get to know your new girlfriend. They're still focused on the family break-up. While you and your husband are living together, it is best to minimize the conflict." Once Ginny has separated and her kids have made some adjustment to their new arrangements, she can begin to deal with her sexuality. The children will begin to understand that Ginny's relationship with her girlfriend is different from other friendships by observing the ways they interact with each other.

If you are living with your husband and developing an open marriage with him, it's often best to be cautious about involving your girlfriend in your children's lives.

I have had a girlfriend for the past seven months. My husband is super understanding and empathetic. She sleeps over almost every Friday night and has dinner with us occasionally. I am a very physical person and like to hug and kiss her (not heavy duty, but little pecks). My eight-year-old daughter is asking pretty benign questions, like how did I meet my girlfriend, but I can see the wheels of her mind turning. How can I normalize this new situation?

— ENID

Enid and her husband are trying out an arrangement that is new to them. It may be confusing to the kids, as Enid is witnessing with her daughter. It is generally better for children to be kept separate from your sexual life. When a woman moves out to be with a girlfriend with whom she expects to create a marital-type relationship, honesty and appropriate affection will help the children understand the situation. In this case, Enid continues to live with her husband and her children do not understand her new behavior. In such cases, if possible, you should keep overnight visits out of your house. Some women have difficulty slowing down because of their excitement. They want the whole world to know about their happiness or they may believe they are ready for a life-long commitment. It is usually best to give yourself time to decide how you and your husband plan to handle your extramarital relationships and how you intend to teach your kids about this. If you are just coming out to yourself, you need time to fully understand how this change will affect you and your marriage. Will this kind of arrangement work for both you and your husband as a way of life? Such questions may need to be answered before you involve the children.

When you are past the honeymoon phase, feel certain that the relationship with your girlfriend is long term and you are spending most of your time together, your children will need to hear your explanation. I told my seven and nine-year old girls that my girlfriend and I loved each other the same way a married couple does. I didn't hide appropriate intimacy with my girlfriend. They saw us hug and kiss affectionately and knew that we slept together. With most children of this age, you need to keep in mind that the most important struggles for them will be to accept the changes occurring between their mother and father. Our new relationship will become natural to them soon enough because they are so young.

If you are in a relationship with a woman who is known to your children in some other role, you will need to decide when and how to tell them about the nature of your involvement. Tamara's girlfriend is a teacher and youth group leader to her three grown children. They have formed their own relationships with her girlfriend and feel affection toward her. Tamara writes:

> I feel like such a bad person for having an affair, especially with someone so involved in my kids' lives. It was so wrong. Can we ever make it right?
>
> — TAMARA

While it is important to understand how your affair has affected the children, it is also important to find a way to forgive yourself— for the affair, for your choice of partner, or for disrupting their lives. If the children loved your girlfriend before finding out about the nature of your relationship, with time, they are likely to eventually find their way back to those feelings. Tamara needs to work through her self-recrimination to prepare herself to talk to her children.

How Do I Handle My Boys?

> How do I let my seven- and eight- year-old boys know that I am a lesbian? They are so very impressionable. I feel like I don't want them to think that I prefer women to men in a way that will make them feel badly about being male.
>
> — TESS

Your children learn the most from the example you set. If you talk and act respectfully toward men, they will not feel that you hate men or their masculinity. This is an ongoing process. There are many teaching opportunities that will come up where you can let them know your feelings. You don't need to have the perfect words, because your love will be communicated and will be the most helpful way to demonstrate that you cherish them as boys. Regardless of conflict between you and your husband, try not to express your anger about him to the kids. If your husband isn't showing you the same respect, explain to the kids that he is angry and really shouldn't talk that way. It helps the children to know that you want them to love both their father and you, thus avoiding loyalty conflicts.

How Do I Handle Difficult Reactions?

I just told my daughter, Cara, today, and it has torn me up inside. She told me she hates me. She wants me to stay in the family that I started even if I'm miserable. She's twenty-one years old, and doesn't understand at all. Of course, we've had the perfect marriage/family/house/cars/kids/dogs/cats, etc., so this has blindsided her. I'm a wreck.

— TANYA

If you are faced with the fear of losing your child's love, as Tanya was, try to find a trusted person to talk to. This will help you to avoid placing all of your anxiety on your child. Give her the space to work through her own feelings. You may expect, or at the very least hope, that she will be understanding because she is a young adult. Even adult children have strong reactions. They sometimes want to protect their father if they see him as a victim and not functioning well. One of my clients decided not to tell her college-aged daughter about her love affair or her plan to leave her marriage because she knew that her daughter would give up her own life to take care of her dad. My client felt that she couldn't live with herself if her daughter did that.

Let your older child know you understand her feelings. When she is ready, try to talk to her about how difficult this process has been for you, and that you would not intentionally hurt her or her father. If you give her the message that you are willing to talk to her more about this when she is ready, on her own time, she is more likely to come to acceptance. If you talk about your change in a positive light, it will help the kids. Don't leave it up to them to bring it up. It may be just as difficult for them to confront the truth and they may never bring it up. It is important to recall how long you have been working this out for yourself. It will take your kids time to grasp and accept this change. If you keep the lines of communication open, most children will eventually come to an understanding.

If you are planning to come out to your child, begin by imagining all possible reactions. It is helpful to prepare yourself for almost anything. First reactions are not usually permanent reactions. Most people need time to digest the information and to understand it. Allow for possible anger, hurt, or even silence. Each can be difficult. As you prepare for a range of possible responses, try not to allow a pattern of emotional abuse to develop. People have a right to their own feelings, but they don't have a right to be cruel. You can let your children know that they have every right to their own feelings, but they cannot treat you with rudeness or cruelty. If they want to talk to you about their feelings, including anger, try not to be defensive; be willing to hear it. Hopefully they will learn to listen to you in return. Preteens and teens may give the appearance of not hearing you, but your words are on the record. All of this effort is about creating an environment for an open exchange of thoughts and feelings. Offering them understanding goes a long way toward setting this up.

If any of your children has a bad reaction, be respectful of their feelings and concerns, but be cautious about allowing their reactions to change your decisions. They will learn about strength, conviction, and self-respect by observing your ability to stay true to yourself without forcing their involvement. One client of mine separated from her husband and moved in with her lover. Her move was slow, and she talked a great deal with her daughters. One of her daughters held on to her anger about the break-up and chose to live with her father. She viewed her father as a victim, and he did little to change that perception. Over the course of two years, her daughter gradually began to talk to her and to rebuild their relationship.

You need to draw upon your patience when facing negative reactions, as it is tempting to fall into the trap of self-hatred or self-condemnation. You might begin to wonder whether you made the wrong decision. Try to confront your own negative thinking by making a list of all the possible benefits and positive lessons your children will learn from your decisions. Remind yourself of this list whenever you catch yourself focusing on regrets.

What If My Husband Uses the Kids Against Me?

It is heartbreaking to talk to women who want only the best for their children but are undermined by vindictive, uncooperative husbands. Children can get caught in the crossfire when one spouse uses them as a weapon to hurt the other spouse. When a parent speaks badly about the other one in the children's presence, the kids suffer. At a time when they most need the love and comfort of both mother and father, they will usually feel abandoned if told that their mother doesn't care anymore or is leaving them. One woman's husband repeatedly told his son that his mother was preventing him from contacting the son. In reality his father wasn't making time to see him. Their child became the victim of their battle. He felt and acted angry at his mom and became desperately upset about visiting his dad. As hard as it is, you cannot protect your child from all of the hurtful behavior that comes his way. At a later time in this child's life, he may examine his father's behavior and reach his own conclusions about the way he was fathered.

Some men create homophobia in their children as a way of distancing them from their mother. Speaking disparagingly in any way about the other parent is something to avoid. You needn't lie to your children or make excuses for your husband, but it is important to work out your anger at him with other people and not in the presence of the kids. They need the freedom to love both parents.

How Do I Help My Children Cope with My Decision to Divorce?

At almost any age, when children learn about their parents' decision to divorce, it is extremely upsetting. With love and support, they will survive and adjust. When custody decisions are made with the children's best interest in mind, kids usually thrive. It takes tremendous emotional and spiritual strength to let go of the personal battles with your husband and even of your dreams and expectations in order to give your children what is best for them.

I am not willing to share my children. I am not willing to wake up in a different place from them. I am not willing to only be there on my "joint custody days." I'm not sure I will ever get to that point until they are much older and more independent (they're four and six now). I listen to other women say that they moved on and gave their husbands custody and I truly cannot comprehend such an action. I will do whatever it takes to be where my children are for as long as I have to, even if it means sacrificing my own happiness.

—BEATRICE

Beatrice's reluctance to give up any part of parenting is a natural and common feeling for mothers. She speaks of trading her happiness for the continuation of full-time parenting. It is important to explore the reasons behind these feelings: Is she afraid of the effects of shared custody on children, worried about losing her role as mother, determined not to hand the children's care to her husband . . .? If you have similar struggles, inform yourself about child custody options and about how to include your own happiness in the decision. An unhappy parent is not a good model for the children and can even create depression in the kids. It may help you to explore: How realistic are your fears? Will such a sacrifice be in the best interest of the children?

My divorce was fairly smooth. I often talked about my parents' divorce and how well they handled it, so we didn't have a negative view to start. We both agreed that I worked at home and had more time for the kids, so it would be better for them to live with me full-time. However, he can arrange to be with the kids any time he wants to. We are lucky that we are friends. We share the kids fairly and equally.

— JEANETTE

Parents maintain a better relationship when divorce and custody arrangements feel fair to both of them. Many women continue having contact and making childrearing decisions with their ex-husbands for years after divorce, so it is important to keep the channels of communication open and positive.

Usually at least one of the parents eventually gets remarried or partnered. Your attitude and your spouse's attitude toward a new union will influence the post divorce environment. Jeanette continued:

My husband met a woman three months after our divorce, and they married a year later. She is great with our kids, and I am mature enough to let my daughter love their stepmom without me feeling threatened. I know she does not replace me, but she is a part of my kid's extended family. Fortunately, my husband is not homophobic, so he has no problem with my living with my girlfriend. My kids love her, too.

— JEANETTE

With a new family arrangement, you are again challenged to let go of previous expectations and of control. Your husband and his new wife may have different rules for the children and different styles of parenting. At first, I found it terribly painful to hear about the problems that my children confronted at their father's house. They were caught in the battles between their father and his new wife, who arrived with three of her own kids. I learned to listen, tried not to overreact, and did some problem-solving with them. Your new partner will also join your family with her own expectations and attitudes about parenting. In the best of circumstances, each parent tries to respect differences and stay consistent with their own parenting approach.

When your kids face problems in your ex-husband's household, let him and his partner work them out. However, you can help your children by talking to them and supporting them if they bring the problems to you. You can offer ideas of how to handle themselves in their other home.

In most cases, rather than intervene, try to help them to talk to their father directly. If there is a parenting issue for which he is responsible, your involvement may be required. For instance, I called my ex-husband to remind him to give the kids money for school or to tell them when he or his wife would be getting home. For the most part, when you hear complaints from the kids, exercise caution about getting involved in the decisions or battles in the other family. Your job is to help your children to become assertive about their needs.

What Are the Kids' Concerns?

At different ages, kids will have different concerns about your disclosure. Yet across the board, children of all ages generally have reactions to the possible end of the marriage, the end of their family as they have known it. On the one hand, children are influenced in ways similar to you regarding what can happen when a family breaks up. They may worry about being abandoned by either parent, about their lives dramatically changing, or about losing the predictability of their future. On the other hand, if your marriage has been very troubled, and they have felt it, they may actually be relieved to anticipate a happier life for either or both parents.

If your children are young, up to preteen, they are likely to grow up seeing two women together as natural if you are comfortable with your sexuality. Once my own children adjusted to the marital separation, they witnessed my new relationship, the affection and happiness, and gradually accepted it as nothing more or less than an intimate relationship. The concerns of an adolescent child may be, "Am I going to be gay?" or "Do you want me to be gay?" You don't have to wait for these questions; just give them your reassurance that most children of gay parents are heterosexual, but you will be happy and accepting of them regardless of their sexual preference. The area in which kids generally need the most help is dealing with the cultural homophobia that we all have to handle. While there have been tremendous improvements in many schools and communities regarding attitudes about LGBT issues, in many places homophobia is still the norm. If you keep the avenues of discussion open to them, they are more likely come to you when they encounter problems.

You may try to run interference for your child in an effort to protect him from homophobia. There is no way to fully insulate your kid, nor would it be helpful to block him from the reality of our homophobic culture. Sometimes a painful situation offers unique opportunities for teaching.

> *My nine-year-old daughter has a best friend. Her mother will not allow her to sleep over at my partner's and my house. Prior to my marital separation, this woman and I were both actively involved in PTA and our kids' sports, etc. I have politely tried to encourage her to understand different points of view, but because of her Catholic beliefs, she will not budge.*
>
> — FRANCES

Words cannot express how painful it is to see your child face homophobia. Frances has attempted to help her daughter first by trying to talk to the other adult. In a situation like this, you can provide the other adults with important information and resources and at least dialogue about homosexuality. But, as I told Frances, "You can lead a horse to water, but you can't make her drink." After a failed attempt, I would back off and move more indirectly.

You may want to help your child understand what homophobia is, so that she can learn that it is a problem in our culture, not a personal failing. Try to talk about homophobia in terms she can understand. For example, a nine-year-old would understand, "Each person has a right to live and behave as he or she wants, as long as other people aren't intentionally hurt. My partner and I love each other the same way married men and women love each other. Some people are prejudiced toward other people who seem different, whether it is racial, religious, or economic differences." You might give examples of prejudice your child has seen in other situations.

When you talk to your child, it's helpful to express pride in your own process. Your children will learn from it. My kids loved my partner, Judy, pretty quickly. She was warm and embracing and far more playful with them than I was. But they had followed me into a new culture. Some of the women they met looked different from the women they knew in the suburban neighborhood where they were raised. Some of my new friends were butch in appearance and weren't confined to gender-stereotypical interests or professions. They included electricians, carpenters, and computer engineers, as well as social workers and teachers. This was quite different from the more traditionally feminine, stay-at-home moms they knew from their limited experiences. At first, they felt uncomfortable with those differences, but their world and tolerance for difference just began to expand.

When they entered adolescence, my kids didn't want my partner, Judy, present at many of their school events because they wanted to hide the nature of our relationship. They were perfectly comfortable at home, but not in their high school environment. This issue often created conflict between Judy and me. As the children's mother, I felt protective of them and their need to adjust to our changes. My partner had been open about her lesbian identity for seven years when we first met. She sometimes felt their shame and avoidance as a personal affront. She devoted a lot of time and energy to helping the kids, and was hurt when they seemed ashamed of her in school settings. I felt the sadness of everyone's struggle and a pressure to try to make it better for all.

Despite our different reactions, Judy and I agreed that the kids were facing many changes, and we tried not to pressure them into acceptance of our lifestyle at a speed that they couldn't handle.

Because of peer pressure, it took them until they were out of high school to come to a comfortable way of integrating their lesbian parents into their social world. My daughters often chose to take their friends home to their father's traditional family environment rather than our house, although they never talked directly about their avoidance of bringing friends into our lives because they didn't want to hurt our feelings. Children generally feel just as protective toward their parents' feelings as we do toward their feelings.

Kids in high school can be brutal, and my daughters wanted to avoid the teasing that might result if they revealed my lesbian relationship. Yet all of their friends knew my partner, and many of them came to their own conclusions over time. When each of the kids left our small community and went to college, they began to feel a desire to come out about my sexuality. Once they found the courage to talk openly to their friends and acquaintances about their family, they developed an intense pride about my partner's and my relationship. Each time a person comes out to another, she is able to lessen her internalized sense of shame. Your children too, will likely develop a deep respect for you if you hold on to the principles of listening carefully to their concerns and respecting their individual timelines for acceptance, while staying true to yourself.

Ironically, some higher power watching over my children offered them a surprise entry into the larger world. By pure chance or fate, each of my daughters went off to a different college and was assigned a freshman roommate whose mother happened to be a lesbian.

WHAT YOU CAN DO NOW

Remind yourself: Taking care of your own happiness is essential to the foundation of successful parenting.

Ask yourself this question: What kind of relationship have you had with your children previously? How will this help or hinder your ability to handle them at this juncture in your life? Is there something you can do at this time to promote better communication?

Practice this technique for handling feelings: Move! Any kind of physical activity will help you to release stress and anxiety. Of course, you have heard this before, and when you are feeling depressed, it is especially hard to follow through. If you have a dog, take him for a walk. If you live in a safe area, walk around the block. If not, get in your car and go somewhere. Change your environment. Begin to associate difficult feelings with the antidote of body movement. It works.

Take one step: Write a letter (one that will never be sent) to one of your children revealing your current situation. Decide how much you should tell and how best to explain according to the age of your child. See this as an exercise that is intended to help you clarify your feelings and decisions. Evaluate your ability to communicate this information to your child in a positive light.

CHAPTER 8

YOUR OPTIONS

Your views about different lifestyles, sexual preferences, marriage, and personal values are the foundation for planning the next chapter of your life. Is your only choice whether to stay or to leave your marriage? When you start to explore your attraction to women, it's difficult to envision any other options. In reality, women find many different solutions to their dilemma. If you can imagine a solution, then it's a possibility. The options available to you depend on your priorities and circumstances, as well as the attitudes of the people intimately involved with you. This is an important time to expand your experience, your knowledge, and even your imagination.

What Are Your Options?

The following vignettes taken from married women's experiences illustrate a range of possibilities.

In-House Separation

> *My husband and I have agreed to stay together until the oldest goes to school next year. We live together, run the house, and do some things together as a family. He has begun to "branch out," and I am free to see my girlfriend. Our priority remains with the kids' well-being in all aspects of life.*
>
> — MAIDIE

Maidie has only tried this for a few months. With this choice, her children and family can continue operating with minimal disruption to the family routines, for the time being. However, Maidie says it feels "schizophrenic" to her; she feels like she is operating with her feet in both worlds. Her decision takes potential pressure off of her children, but Maidie doesn't know whether she can keep up the front for a whole year.

A woman named Tasha negotiated an in-house separation with her husband in order to share the care of their severely disabled child. They had a large house that allowed each of them to live independently and to establish new intimate relationships for themselves. The time consuming management of their child was their primary focus. New partners in either of their lives have to be comfortable with the other spouse's involvement and the centrality of their childcare. You may have your own reason for needing to maintain the same living space with your husband. Such arrangements require good communication, flexibility, and some emotional detachment.

Waiting for the Kids to Leave

> *My girlfriend of three years severed our relationship recently. I had been feeling very guilty leaving the kids to spend time with*

*her. I feel I must sacrifice so my children will be happy. I have set
a goal to stay with my husband until both kids leave home in
five years. In the meantime, I feel lonely and miss the intimacy.*
— ALENA

Alena's situation differs from Maidie's in-house separation primarily in the length of her wait. It is Alena's belief that her children
come first and that a divorce would harm them. She feels it is necessary to put her personal needs to the side until the kids leave home.
Several factors will affect the outcome of this decision: the quality
and peacefulness of the marriage, the length of waiting time, and
how the delay affects either spouse's emotional state. If the time
period is a year or less, most women find a way to handle the delay.
You can use the time to prepare for upcoming changes: finding
housing, handling financial matters, consulting with an attorney, etc.

If you plan to wait a few years before leaving, be alert to problems with your children. Dena contacted me about her ten-year old
daughter, who was having problems in school with her peers. Her class
grades had fallen and she was dropping hints that she was worried
her parents might get divorced. Children often have an uncanny perception of family problems. If you don't talk to them about the marital problems and they sense them, they will not feel free to talk about
what they are feeling. You may need to reconsider your timing in order
to help your children deal directly with their unspoken anxieties.

What women often claim is their greatest obstacle to making a
dramatic change is their concern for their children. But it's essential
at this juncture that you make sure that you recognize the importance of your own priorities. Deferring your own needs and focusing primarily on others often leads to depression. Your impulse to
put your children first is understandable, but if you're depressed
they could end up struggling with depression too. It's vital that you

include your happiness in the equation for balancing your family's well-being.

Waiting to Divorce for Other Reasons

Children aren't the only reason for delaying a separation or divorce. You may have made the decision to pursue a different way of life, but the inability to take care of yourself or your children in any way can affect the timing of your plans.

> I'm working on becoming more financially stable in hopes of moving into a home near my husband and kids. We agreed that the marriage was over two years ago, and I've been dating women exclusively since. I know that as long as I'm financially dependent on my husband and living under the same roof, filing for divorce would do more harm than good. What friendship we have left would shatter in that instant.
>
> — INGRID

Women often feel that they have emotionally separated from their husbands when they get involved in a lesbian community and start to date. You may find, as Ingrid did, that there are limits to being fully involved in either your marriage or your new lesbian life. Ingrid has difficulty explaining her physical arrangement to other women whom she dates. Whatever keeps you dependent on your husband keeps you tied to him. Sometimes it's impossible to leave until you have the means for self-sufficiency. In such cases, you need to accept that you are not fully unencumbered and "free" to start a new life. In fact, you are still preparing for your future as long as your marital separation is not complete.

Maintaining Your Marriage and Your Girlfriend

My husband hopes our marriage won't end; he's fine with my having a girlfriend. He, my girlfriend, and I have talked about working this out as a threesome, not in the same house, but in a way that would not involve totally abandoning my husband. The thought of just dumping him is abhorrent to me. I no longer have a sexual relationship with him, but I do feel a strong emotional and family tie to him.

—VICKY

Such an arrangement usually works if your husband is supportive and all three of you benefit in some way from your extramarital relationship. The advantage for both you and your husband may be simply that you can hold on to the marriage. Your husband may be experiencing a happier wife, which improves the quality of his life. Vicky's husband realizes he can't provide the intensity or intimacy that his wife seeks. He feels less pressured when his wife is satisfied and, therefore, less demanding of him. Vicky finds that she is less angry at her husband because she is now getting her needs met. She prefers to stay married because of the familiarity and comfort of the life she has built with her husband. Her girlfriend has a time-consuming job and likes the freedom of this arrangement.

However, even when all three participants agree to the arrangement, problems often arise when the relationship between any two of the participants deepens. As soon as one person wants more, the balance is upset. That's when married women often feel pressured to make a choice. Additionally, the effort to keep husband and girlfriend happy can be very stressful for a married woman. One woman wrote that she is involved with a woman she met online. From the start, her girlfriend knew she was committed to her marriage. She and her girlfriend live in different states and meet every month some place away from each of their homes. They all seem to be happy. She explained, "My husband sees a difference in our relationship. I have grown, my husband has grown, and my girlfriend feels fulfilled."

Some married couples prefer a more balanced arrangement where both husband and wife are free to have outside relationships. This kind of agreement seems to work when both spouses' needs are met by another partner. While a husband and wife may begin their trial arrangement with certainty that they want to stay together forever, as either of the extramarital relationships deepen, the couple's original bonds often weaken. It is impossible to anticipate how your needs may change as you evolve. One client became overwhelmed with sadness whenever thinking about what might happen to her marriage. She was unable to predict that her feelings toward her marriage would change. Over time she and her husband grew more distant, but she discovered she was prepared to face the possible dissolution of her marriage as she became closer to her lover.

Women who define themselves as bisexual sometimes feel unfulfilled if they don't have a relationship with both a man and a woman in some ongoing way. Other bisexuals feel equal attractions, but are content to commit to one person without missing involvement with the other sex. Those who have a need for dual involvements often have difficulty fitting into any community. Neither the straight nor the lesbian community has much understanding or tolerance for a married woman seeking a woman lover, and many bisexual groups seem to be focused more on sex and experimentation. This is a frustrating experience that requires patience and creativity in order to arrive at a solution.

I am 100 percent bisexual. I don't think I would be totally happy if I just had the one sex in my life. What some people don't real-ize is that some bisexuals have a real need to have both sexes. It is a need, not just a desire. I met my girlfriend via the internet. It took a lot of wading through people, but I narrowed it down when I decided that it would be best to have a relationship with a woman as similar to me as possible, i.e., a married bisexual with children whose husband was aware of her sexuality.

—DARLA

As Darla writes more, you sense the fragility of the balance required to keep each person satisfied. Yet this arrangement works well for now. If it becomes unsatisfactory, they may have to recon-sider their decisions. Many decisions work for a while and must be reworked if or when one partner's feelings change.

At the moment everyone seems to be happy. My husband doesn't have to come home to a wife who is "breaking down"' and depressed all the time. Our sex life has actually improved, and so has hers with her husband. I had a lot of therapy. I did a lot of thinking; it was extremely hard. I'm waiting for the bubble to burst, but for now I am happy and hopeful. At the end of the day, I don't want to choose between the sexes. I am who I am, I can't help that.

—DARLA

Most women who get involved with another woman while mar-ried do so secretly at first. Some wonder if it is possible to maintain a marriage and an ongoing secret relationship with another woman. Almost anything is possible. If you are considering this option, examine the underlying reasons. You will pay a price if you made this choice in response to fear or internalized homophobia. Sydney's message suggests both. Maintaining secrets will undermine the integrity of your marriage. Fear of discovery and shame may also become an integral part of the extramarital relationship.

My girlfriend and I are deeply in love and committed to each other on all levels. We are both married to terrific guys. I don't believe that either of us could EVER "go public," and even if we could, we have an additional dilemma: my best friend/lover has been a teacher for each of my children and a dear family friend. We are both leaders in our church. I truly believe we can continue this intimate relationship "in-secret."

— **SYDNEY**

By keeping her extramarital relationship secret, Sydney maintains the image and lifestyle that she has established with her husband and family. However, she loses the possibility for honesty and intimacy in all her other relationships, including family, children, and friends. These decisions come down to prioritizing values. This is not an easy task. Religion, community life, and family acceptance are not simple issues to confront or to alter. Your priorities and your coping skills are the key to whether this option can work for you.

Recommitting to Your Marriage

I decided to recommit to my marriage (also helped by a loving supportive husband). Although it is hard to know I will never be able to explore this part of my sexuality, I believe that what I am gaining is far more than what I am losing. In fact, I am still a les-

bian, and I have friends who understand that and with whom I can express my lesbian identity. But I won't do anything that will jeopardize what I have with my husband and kids.

— KIM

While exploring her sexuality, Kim felt that she was making different decisions with every new day. Something changes when you decide to put your heart into a decision. The plan may or may not be final, but you know you are giving it a sincere attempt. Rekindling the positive aspects of your marriage entails hard work, and much of the work will focus on you. Happiness doesn't come just from another person, but from discovering your internal sources of joy. It's possible that some sexual needs or desires may go unmet when you refocus on the marriage. Kim added, "Sometimes I feel desire that I can't act upon, but I guess anyone trying to be monogamous would feel the same."

Some women feel it would be a conflict to hold onto their lesbian identity but not pursue the lifestyle. In the following message, Martha has made the same decision as Kim, but believes that hers is still a part of the exploration process:

I've taken a few forays out into the lesbian world, and it's like coming home to myself. I never imagined that I could feel so comfortable and happy. I always thought I was innately insecure and unsettled. Not so. Yet my husband and children are also supremely important, so it is not as simple as following my inner desires. I am at peace with the decision to stay in my marriage and to just be with the struggle of seeing where this goes.

—MARTHA

If you have been involved with a girlfriend for several months or years, the decision to recommit to marriage can be an arduous and lengthy struggle. You will grieve the loss of your lover. When you set a goal to work out the marriage, it's best to protect your husband from the full intensity of the grief. Try to get your support from a therapist or trusted friends or family members. Letting go of someone you love and of the dreams connected to her sometimes takes several years to fully resolve. If this is your choice, you must be patient and make the most of the moments of peace and happiness that occur while you are healing. Unless you have kept your sexuality hidden, this decision requires a supportive husband.

I came out to my husband about a year ago. He said he suspected it and still loves me. I have chosen to stay with him, because I do love him. However, it is a different kind of marriage. We are best friends and get along very well. Since our kids are grown, we aren't staying together for the kids. It's something that most people don't understand. I am not staying because I don't have the money to leave. This is my way of putting my family first, and, in the process, it is a very satisfying and joyous life!

— **ANDREA**

Other women who decide to stay married do so without a feeling of compromise. After thorough exploration of their situations, they conclude that they are heterosexual. Clarinda reached this conclusion.

I spent a lot of time trying to determine what my true sexual identity is. While I love my friend and truly enjoyed spending every moment with her that I did, I believe it was just her. I fell in love with a person, regardless of her gender. I do not long for or feel a need to make a lifestyle change in order to be true to myself. I enjoy being with my husband intimately, and life has improved so much for me, for us. My friend has moved on in her own life, finding a woman she is happy with. My husband and I were meant to be together. It has been almost two years of ups and downs, but so worth the process to be where we are now.

— CLARINDA

Living Independent of Any Relationship

Immediately following divorce, women often need time to live independently. The dissolution of a marriage is extremely complicated emotionally, practically, and spiritually. You may be conflicted between your goal of finding a life partner and your need for separateness and healing. I may have been lucky that my first girlfriend ended our relationship. When I left my husband, I was single, but not alone. I focused on getting to know the lesbian community, making new friends, meeting women, and dating. Sometimes the fear of ending up alone causes women to rush into the search for a special woman. It's important to reserve time to get to know your emerging self. Lauren describes her experience:

Here I sit, ten months into separation, not involved with anyone, both happy and sad about that. I really don't want a relationship right now, but boy, would I like to play around. What a gift to myself to finally feel my feelings! I'm not quite over the loss of the dreams associated with my marriage, nor am I over the negatives of that relationship. The flip side is that waiting is sometimes boring, sometimes maddening. Will I ever want to be in a relationship again?

— LAUREN

You may not choose to live independently, but circumstances may lead you there. Many women who try to move directly from marriage into a lesbian relationship discover that they can't give the new relationship their full attention. If your relationship dissolves, your unplanned aloneness doesn't have to be lonely. This situation may motivate you to reach out into the lesbian community for friendship and support. Even if you didn't choose it, time alone offers you an opportunity to develop your self-sufficiency.

Up until two weeks ago I was with someone. We stopped seeing each other because she wanted more; I wanted less. Not sure why. So here I am, forty-one, in an apartment, experiencing aloneness for the first time in my life. Not bad. I am learning to take care of myself. I am learning that the fear of something is usually worse than the actual something.

— TINA

Marital Separation

Marital separation can have different purposes. It can be a way to create space to make important decisions and allow time for introspection. Alternatively, it can be the first step toward divorce. Try to be honest with yourself about your intentions when proposing a separation. If you are on a path toward ending your marriage, be as clear as possible with your husband and children. Separation is not advisable in most cases when a wife and husband are trying to work on their marriage. If you are separating in order to have pressure-free time, be careful not to undermine that goal by spending all of your free time with your girlfriend or by staying so busy that you don't have time to think.

My husband moved out two weeks ago and I miss him so much. I miss both him and our family being together. My depression has gotten better since he's moved out, but when I see him, I don't want him to leave.

— MJ

When you separate, begin to set goals for how you would like to use the time. You may feel like MJ, that you miss your husband and family life. Losing someone so important to you creates a void. You need to acknowledge that emptiness and grieve, but also recognize that you must discover other sources of happiness. Pay attention to your feelings; they may help guide you. Sadness related to loss is normal, but depression is not helpful. Since MJ regularly feels depressed after visiting with her husband, she might benefit from seeing him less often. If the depression doesn't lift over time, she may need to reevaluate her decision. One woman offered advice concerning the natural grieving process that occurs with separation:

You will find that there are days that you will slip back and wonder if you did the right thing . . . and wonder if you can live this lifestyle. But remember that no matter what happens, you are who you are now, and you have to accept that. You will grieve your past and your marriage for a long time. You are doing what you have to do in order to be true to yourself . . . just take it in stages and try to close one chapter at a time.

— MERRY

Both separation and divorce are sometimes negotiated in an atmosphere of caring and friendship. If you and your husband can talk openly and plan to share parenting, it makes sense to try to maintain good feelings as long as they don't reflect lack of separation or interfere with new relationships. Dale describes her separation as unconventional:

When I moved out of our marriage bed, my husband asked for a divorce. We sold our large house and each bought separate homes. I am living with my female partner, and he has a very accepting lover of his own. We wanted to stay close by because I still have a high schooler at home and because I do still care about my husband. Although my partner has accepted my friendship with my husband, she has set her own boundaries. She doesn't want to be friends with him and expects him to respect the sanctity of our home, i.e., no dropping over without calling.

— DALE

Reconciling after a Separation

It takes a good deal of insight to understand the reasons behind a desire for reconciliation with your husband. Just as you need to take time to make effective decisions regarding divorce, you need the same for contemplating a return to your husband. Is your desire to reunite actually an attempt to cut off your grief process, or have you learned something new about yourself while taking steps to develop a different life? The amount of time you have given to your adjustment will help you to answer this question. It takes some women longer than others to let go of their losses. You may not appreciate what you have now until you have finished that process. Pay attention to what you are telling yourself. Your self-talk offers the best information about the meaning of your change of heart. Anna Mae's following message suggests that she may have separated prematurely from her husband. She did not work through her guilt and shame, and is seeing the undermining effects that often result.

I am trying to find a way to return to my marriage after two-and-a-half years in a relationship with a woman whom I have loved and still love deeply. I haven't been able to tell anyone of this relationship, and I have never been able to close the door on my marriage totally. I love my husband but not with passion or desire, but know I have to try to build this back into my relationship with him. Can I find a way back? Is there any one who has done this and made a success of it?

— ANNA MAE

You may have tried to do something that you were not truly ready to do. This is still part of your exploration process. When you refocus on your husband, it's common to go through a grieving process in relation to your girlfriend. With time, you will know more clearly which decision is best for you.

Divorce

Commitment is important. I know that. I was committed for nineteen years. However, I am not the same person today. I hope to teach my children that no one else is in charge of your happiness and you are not in charge of anyone else's. You always have a choice. It is better to be <u>from</u> a broken home than <u>in</u> one.

— PATRICE

Patrice's beliefs come after a long period of questioning. There are many different reasons women decide to divorce. Some feel they cannot sacrifice their life for other people; some feel it is the only way that they can be authentic. Others make this decision to be fair to both themselves and their husbands, who, they believe, deserve more in life.

The disadvantages of divorce are quite clear for most women considering this option. There are so many tasks, emotional and practical, that must be addressed to dissolve the bonds of marriage that you may not be able to envision a better time.

My husband and I are separated and soon will be filing for divorce. Sometimes I feel happy about the path I've chosen. Other times I miss the comfort of my old life. I know I am griev-ing over the loss of a life that is no more. I expected that since this was my decision that it should only be my husband who is mourning, but that is not the case.

— JOHANNA

Grieving has little to do with how right your decision is. Some people experience enormous grief when they separate; others feel a sense of relief. Many feel both. Your response to divorce may be related to how quickly you came to the decision or how much prep-aration you did before your move. Many women feel that the time of exploration and decision-making is so excruciating that finally mak-ing a decision becomes a turning point.

The Divorce Process

If you plan to divorce, you will need to negotiate the legal sys-tem. Finding and communicating your needs to an attorney can be challenging. You must be your own advocate, perhaps for the first time. Your attorney may want to take a harder line than feels com-fortable to you. Or she may suggest giving away what feels important to you. For instance, I felt that the first lawyer I hired didn't firmly represent my interests in the way I wanted. He encouraged me to accept almost every offer from my husband, which led me to believe that he wasn't taking my concerns seriously. While I appreciated his stress on finding solutions that would avoid major battles, his goal seemed to outweigh an interest in trying to see my perspective. So I found another lawyer who seemed to understand me better. Whenever you seek professional help, it is essential that you feel understood and can trust that your lawyer has your best interests in mind. You don't have to be ready for divorce to learn about your rights. Schedule a consultation with an attorney to educate yourself about your custody rights, your financial rights, and ways to protect your interests. Knowing your rights will empower you.

I almost gave up custody. At the time I FELT like a horrible mother. I felt guilty about their dad not having the kids in his life 24 hours a day. I couldn't "see" my "new" life merging with being a good mother. It has and I am.

— MERCEDES

Women generally choose either a mediator or a lawyer to handle divorce. In either case, your feelings of guilt can undermine your best intentions. Women who feel responsible for the breakup may give up their rights and ask for less than they truly deserve or need. Mercedes wrote further about her inability to imagine how things might change for her in the future when she was negotiating her divorce.

I left and signed mostly everything over to the ex and left the kids with him also. Do I regret it? Yes, I do. It wasn't too long before I really started missing being part of their lives. Now I have to go to court and fight for visitation rights (which I also agreed to very little of). I was caught up in all the new emotions of my newfound love (who left me after eight months). I regret a lot of what I've done. I should have thought things out more than I did.

If you are caught up in the excitement of a new relationship, you may need a professional to help you look at the long-term implications of your decisions. Mediators focus on avoiding contentious litigation by coming to mutual agreements. However, mediation requires two spouses willing to negotiate in this way. Lawyers represent the individual and work to make sure you don't give up your rights.

Adjusting to Divorce

It takes time to adjust to the changes and the emotions that accompany divorce. You may feel confused by your reactions and even uncertain about your decisions. If you are having trouble adjusting, it is essential to allow yourself the time and opportunity to explore your reactions. If possible, get some counseling and avoid making any major moves for at least a year.

I felt I had to leave because of my newfound feelings with my girlfriend. I have been very in love with her but now wonder if I can do this forever. My old life is haunting me. The rejection of friends, family, and society is saddening me so much. I have not spoken of my feelings to my husband or my girlfriend. I find myself looking at him and thinking how handsome he is and how wonderful he was to me. I am quiet and unsure of so much.
— JOY

If you really have made a mistake, you can explore with your husband the possibility of reconciling, but remember that it is normal to feel regrets. When you are grieving, you sometimes only remember the good times. Make a list of both the good points and the reasons why you left your marriage. If possible, get involved with your local lesbian community and work on building friendships. It's natural for your feelings to fluctuate. Try to avoid impulsive decisions. It's best to allow yourself to feel your sadness and your discomfort. Avoid making yet another change right away and instead focus on working out your feelings. Whatever direction your exploration takes, remember that you are the final judge of what lifestyle fits your needs and desires.

Starting Over, With Your Girlfriend

I know the odds of two married women with children falling in love, actually divorcing, and spending the rest of their lives together is very, very small. But I am a gambler and I'll take that bet.

— KRISTINE

Whether you both are married or just one of you is, there are many hurdles for women who get involved while still married. Kristine feels that the struggles she and her partner have gone through together help them to know that they are fighting for something very precious. She recognizes the difficulties of her choice. She may make mistakes and have some regrets, but she will never know what is possible unless she tries.

Like Kristine, you may feel that you have found the partner with whom you want to build your future. Many women are less certain. You can't predict the outcome of your new relationship. If you leave your husband to be with your partner, you may bypass aspects of the coming out process. Some women feel a need, once they fully acknowledge their attraction to women, to explore different sexual and emotional experiences with other women. In such cases, they may feel stifled by an immediate commitment to a marital-type union with their girlfriend.

Finding Your Own Voice

Until you find your bearings, it is easy to fall prey to the temptation of letting other people choose your direction. Husbands and girlfriends sometimes offer lots of advice.

About a year ago I met a woman. She is now my best friend and also gay. I am totally in love with her, but she doesn't want anything more than a friendship. She wants me to move to California, where she now lives, so that I can live my lifestyle. If I divorce my husband because I am gay, I am worried he will try to take my son from me. I have very low self-confidence and I am not sure what to do.

— ROSE

Gradually it becomes apparent that no one else can tell you what is best for you. Even in therapy, many women hope to be given the answers. A skilled professional will listen to you purposefully and actively so that you will begin to pay attention to what you are saying. Your personal growth will come from within. Your decisions will result from knowing yourself, accepting yourself, and overcoming your fears. Each of the options described in this chapter demonstrates how unique and personal the married woman's choices are.

WHAT YOU CAN DO NOW

Remind yourself: In *Notes on Love and Courage,* Hugh Prather says, "I can't help people by damaging myself. In fact, if it's beginning to destroy me, I can be confident it's not helping them." It's a good idea to check in to see whether your choices are in fact self-destructive or self-nurturing.

Ask yourself this question: As you read about the different paths that women have taken, which ones resonate for you? In answering this question, avoid focusing on the obstacles that immediately come to mind. This exercise is meant to stimulate your imagination and lend credence to your instincts.

Practice this technique for handling feelings: You cannot overcome difficult feelings until you accept them–that they are present and normal for your situation. Using your journal, describe the feeling that is most distressing: guilt, fear, anxiety, sadness . . . What beliefs are feeding into this feeling? For example, when I felt overwhelmed with guilt about hurting my husband, some of my beliefs were as follows: "He has been a good husband and provider. His feelings will always be damaged. He really loves me." Stay with your feeling for several minutes and then write your thoughts about it. Remind yourself at the conclusion of this exercise that these are just feelings and you needn't do anything at this moment to change them. This is an exercise about acceptance.

Take one step: Choose one of the options described in this chapter and make a list of each step that you would need to take in order to make this happen. Identify the first small step and try it out.

CHAPTER 9

EXPANDING YOUR SUPPORT AND RESOURCES

We are all limited by the parameters of our experience. This is especially important to remember when you face any kind of life crisis. You cultivate resilience and resourcefulness by seeking knowledge and community with other people who share your experience. Isolation is a universal experience for married women who are attracted to women because they are caught between two worlds, heterosexual and gay. Neither community seems to understand the issues unique to their situation. The feeling of displacement engendered by isolation often creates uncertainty about whom to trust.

I suddenly don't feel like I fit in anywhere. I still go to dinner, craft night, play cards, etc., with all my friends (most of whom are married), but I suddenly don't want to spend as much time with these people. I do have two good friends who are lesbians whom I talk to, but I feel like I need a circle of friends who are like me.

— JESSIE

There are many channels for developing a new network, including local and internet bookstores, a host of internet resources ranging from online chat groups, blogs, social networks, and message boards, to gay/lesbian/bisexual websites, as well as local support groups and psychotherapy.

While I was desperate for information about lesbianism and alternative lifestyles in 1979, I needed something more. I was searching for inspiration. I attended a lecture by lesbian author Rita Mae Brown, who spoke about the power lesbians gain through visibility—the importance of coming out. I became engrossed in romantic novels about spirited women who lived their lives outside the norms of society, and I was encouraged by hearing about women, fictional or real, who overcame enormous obstacles to become the powerful women they were.

Some women prefer to read about a new subject first. When I was searching for information some thirty years ago, we didn't have the anonymity offered today with online shopping and web surfing. It often felt vulnerable walking into a gay-oriented bookstore or buying a lesbian themed book in a mainstream bookstore. Finding a book on a topic that felt so revealing could be reminiscent of adolescent times, when going to the drugstore for tampons or condoms felt embarrassing (everyone will know why you are there!). Most people today can search the internet bookstores, websites, blogs and other sources of information for almost any concern. If you want to maintain anonymity as you reach out to others, you may start your venture online. Most women who contact me for help start with a quick Google search for "married lesbian or married woman in love with a woman." This kind of search will take you to informational sites and email lists that are devoted to this subject, some more helpful than others. In the Resources section, I offer more details about making use of the Internet. Maria explained the significance of the online contact in her life:

In my real life, I live surrounded by people who I've never been able to share any of my last eight months with, and here on this internet forum, I found the greatest little village of women struggling to find themselves in this race of "WHO am I?", pulling each other along, and hearing the onlookers as they screamed encouraging words along the finish line. I come here for validation and confirmation, that I'm not alone.

— MARIA

It's not necessary to try to handle this transformational experience by yourself. Reaching out may at first seem daunting, but it's generally helpful to actively work to create a community that will support you through your changes. On my internet message board (askjoanne.net), women share their advice about every concern. The following is a response to a question about how to meet other women:

If there is a women's center or GLBT center where you live, they usually know of events, dances, and so on. Also, they often run social and support groups for women who are "coming out." Give them a call! You shouldn't have to give your name or address or anything like that. It should be one hundred percent safe.

— ESTHER

If you are still questioning your sexuality and not certain about exploring a lesbian lifestyle, you may find a coming-out support group premature. Some women feel uncomfortable in a lesbian coming-out group while living in a heterosexual marriage. Their primary concerns are quite different from those of single women. However, if this is the only group available to you, it may provide new friendships and a safe place to talk.

Ultimately nothing takes the place of contact with people: other women facing similar questions, gay men or women who have personal and community information and contacts, mental health professionals, and potentially supportive friends and family. Dialogue with others helps you identify your most important issues and clarify your beliefs and values. As you move forward in this self-discovery process, regardless of your choices, you will need a support network.

In my early attempts to work through the confusion, I discovered that my style of learning was primarily interpersonal. My curiosity was piqued by any woman whom I believed was gay or bisexual. I asked questions I never would have imagined asking of women I barely knew. After attending a work-related conference, I contacted the leader, an open lesbian, to learn about her coming-out experience. When she invited me to the home she shared with her lover, I entered a beautiful apartment with a lovely view of the city. This experience offered me new evidence that lesbians didn't all live on the edge of poverty, as I had suspected. I arranged time with another new acquaintance to hear about her story of leaving home with her five children after a long marriage. Today I don't even remember their names. In retrospect, I realize I was gathering information about how women found the courage to move from the security of marriage into a whole new way of life. I couldn't yet envision any specific changes for myself.

You may feel uncomfortable approaching new acquaintances in this way, and yet I hadn't realized my ability to do this, either. Desperation can compel a person to do things she believes herself incapable of doing. You too may surprise yourself. Don't hesitate to ask your questions, in person, by contacting local agencies, or in cyberspace. Today there are several online discussion boards and email lists that will address your concerns. My "Ask Joanne" online message board welcomes women who are married and questioning their sexuality to talk to each other about topics others in their lives may not understand. In recent years, an increased need for face-to-face contact has led to the informal development of small "AJ" (Ask Joanne) groups that meet socially in various cities around the country. When you reach out either online or in person, you are developing strength to keep yourself moving in your process of transformation.

Jane's questions to other married women on the internet reflect the common need for understanding and some basis for hope:

> *Is there anyone out there who married a wonderful man but always felt a void? Even though you continued to love him? Then you realized that the love of a woman was the void? Did any of you leave your husband because of this? Start over? Start your journey alone? Has anyone done this? And survived emotionally? How long did it take to feel good about your decision?*
>
> — JANE

These questions elicited many personal stories that helped Jane to find courage, if not specific answers.

If you don't have access to the internet or cannot maintain privacy with your computer, then you will need to find another way to make contact. Most urban or university areas have a gay/lesbian center or hotline that lists local resources. These places usually have information on gay/lesbian-friendly therapists for professional support. You might also go to a public library for your initial internet search. Due to the strict confidentiality requirements of the mental health profession, working with a professional in group, couples, or individual therapy is often the safest place to begin a face-to-face dialogue.

Group, Couples, or Individual Therapy?

Therapy and Support Groups

Joining a married women's coming-out support or therapy group is a powerful way to address your issues. It may be worth traveling some distance to become a member of a group if this is accessible to you. The group format offers you the opportunity to confront your solitude by sharing your experience with other women who are facing similar challenges. These groups are most effective when facilitated by an experienced professional who knows how to create a climate of safety. You will benefit from an environment that welcomes the expression of all of your feelings in the course of sharing your story. In the Philadelphia married women's workshops that I conduct, women speak openly about their fears—of disapproval, of what the "gay life-style" entails (and all of the associated myths), of hate-directed violence, of custody battles, of hurting spouses/children/parents, and so on. Participants are free to voice their prejudices without the need to be "politically correct," thereby overcoming concerns they may have never voiced before. They also share their feelings of excitement about new loves, their attractions, and new self-awareness.

Eileen describes the impact of a married women's support group she attended at my office:

When I joined, I was terrified and confused. I came in search of answers. I needed to know that my feelings were real and that even though I never had an inkling in thirty-nine years that I might be gay, I, in fact, might be. I thought there was nobody else as confused or lonely as I was. I never dreamed I could be in a group of women who knew exactly how I felt, but they did . . . because they felt it, too. At first I was overcome by the sadness in the room, but in the end, I not only found solace in that sadness, I found myself.

— EILEEN

Sonya writes about her experience:

We keep coming to these groups to find out others have led "normal" lives like us, only to realize that "normal" is really all about each person's own perspective and what feels comfortable to her.

— SONYA

Groups are not for everyone. If you are very shy or so overwhelmed by your fears that you would be upset hearing about others women's fears, group work is not the place to begin. Consider going first to individual counseling to alleviate your anxiety. A group is helpful only if it leads to a feeling of support, not one of increased fear. If you aren't comfortable sharing or listening to others by the end of the third session of a support group, it is time to try a different approach. The weekend workshop format that I developed usually allows enough structured group time, social time, and alone time that most women find a way to connect with others in the manner that's easiest for them. However, for some people individual or marital therapy may be more effective.

Marriage Counseling

There is a difference between couples and individual therapy, and you need to decide which is best for you. Couples therapy focuses specifically on the marriage; technically, your marriage is the client. If you're considering this kind of professional help, first identify your personal goals. Most couples enter marriage counseling to try to improve their marriage. Occasionally couples therapy is focused on communication about a separation, such as arranging shared parenting or negotiating the details of separation.

I pursued marriage counseling because I needed to know that I was giving the marriage my best effort before making any decisions. My husband and I attended only two sessions before our gifted therapist recognized that we weren't dealing with a couples' issue. I had to decide whether I wanted to recommit to my marriage or to explore a lesbian life. After that point, our therapist met with my husband and me separately for about six months. I focused on making a decision. Our therapist helped my husband to recognize his part in our marital problems so that he would feel less victimized by the situation. We both benefited tremendously from the therapy.

If you are currently involved with a woman and have not revealed this to your husband or have not revealed your same-sex attractions, before you seek marriage counseling ask yourself these questions:

- *What do I hope to accomplish from the therapy?*
- *What you can accomplish is limited if you are holding secrets that affect your marriage?*
- *Do I want to use marriage counseling to help me reveal the truth? This would be a good reason for working with a couples therapist. If you are particularly fearful of your husband's responses, a third party can be helpful in this process.*
- *Have I given my marriage a real chance? Marriage counseling often follows the decision to let go of an extramarital relationship. This type of therapy is best when you want to explore the possibilities for improving your marriage.*

I am living with my husband until we have worked out divorce mediation and some of my own issues. He gave me license to

see my lover as long as he knows when I am coming home.
When I arrived home late one night, he was furious. He said I
am asking him to be either uncomfortable in his own home, or
to set a curfew making him act as if he were my father. I am
confused. Aren't these issues he needs to work out, or is this
something to take to our couples therapist?

— SALLY

Sally's situation is a couples' issue. When you are living with your husband and he knows about your relationship with your lover, you need to define new parameters for your marriage. You and your husband each need to define for the other what you can tolerate under the current circumstances. Individually, each of you needs to continue assessing whether you still want to work on the relationship. As a couple, you are redefining the rules of your marriage, even if temporary. This task must be done together. There are few precedents, so the two of you need to negotiate how to do this in your own way. If Sally and her husband are unable to come to some agreement that both can live with, they might decide to find a way to separate sooner.

If you know that you really don't want to work on improving your marriage, couples therapy will likely be a waste of time and money. There are times when therapy can potentially be counterproductive. If your husband is seeking help to mend the marriage and you are looking for a way out, the therapy will be confusing and may intensify the frustration and anger. In addition, you may be offering your spouse a bit of misguided hope that reinforces his denial of how serious your situation is. For example:

I came out to my husband about six weeks ago, and we have
agreed to stay together at least two more years until our

youngest is out of the house. He knows that after that, I want to move on with my life as a lesbian. This week he told me that he wants to go to couples therapy. I know that the only way this will work is if we both want it to work, and I don't. I'm afraid to hurt him even more in therapy by telling the truth, but I'm afraid that if I don't lay it all out on the table, I will mislead him by going to couples therapy.

— MARGE

Marge's instincts are correct. Therapy can mislead your spouse if you are not very clear about your motives. It is likely that if Marge were to remain open and direct about her plans to leave, her husband would end the therapy after one or two sessions. He may need to be painfully reminded in the presence of a third party in order to accept the reality of their future. If you feel ambivalent about the direction of your marriage, sometimes merely the attempt to work out problems in therapy can result in a better understanding of whether you really want to save your marriage.

Individual Therapy

Some circumstances demand that you find professional help just for yourself. If you are very depressed or agitated, or are resorting to self-destructive habits, a therapist can best offer you guidance. When it looks like there are no answers to your problems, you may fall prey to feelings of helplessness or despair. Following are several messages that indicate a need for professional help:

I have never been so confused in all my life. I feel like I just want to end life. Why does it have to be so hard?

— KIRBY

I have lost that sense of relief and peace I first felt when I realized who I really am. I am once again overeating and have begun drinking more than I should. I know I need to talk this out with someone I can trust.

— GEORGIA

I've come to this place where I feel like, before I move out and change my two children's lives, I need to come more into myself, like myself, have more self-esteem, etc.

— GRETA

If you feel you can't function normally in your daily life or are overwhelmed by emotional swings, you should find a good therapist. However, you don't have to reach a point of complete breakdown to seek therapy. If you have minimal support, therapy can be a safe place to talk to someone who will listen objectively. Individual therapy can also be helpful for sorting through your confusion regarding your sexual identity and what you need in an intimate relationship.

Finding the Right Therapist

After twenty years of therapy, I think I have finally hit on one of the main reasons for my unhappiness: I am lesbian. So why have I spent so much money on therapy? Because I kept skirting the issue of my sexuality. I am finally with a therapist who is helping me face who I am.

— PERRY

It's possible that Perry didn't talk about the issue of sexual identity in her prior therapy because she wasn't ready to confront the conflicts it would raise for her. Or perhaps she hadn't yet found a therapist with whom she felt comfortable. Both ingredients are necessary for doing this vulnerable work. You are exploring core identity concerns. Questions of homosexuality, in particular, often bring up feelings of shame.

There are some basic principles for identifying the right professional to guide you through your journey. No matter what approach a therapist uses, the most important factor in therapy is the trusting relationship that develops between client and therapist. Trust is developed when the therapist is a good listener and helps you feel at ease. He or she should be nonjudgmental, no matter what the issue, and experienced enough to offer insight and direction, not answers. Your therapist should be familiar with gay issues—especially those that married women face—and be able to direct you to appropriate resources in your community.

If you don't live in an urban area, it may be difficult to find a therapist who has this kind of experience. However, if you pay attention to their reactions, you will know whether she or he understands the depth of your struggle. Your intuition and response are your most important guides.

The initial connection with my therapist was the deciding factor for me. That connection was started by the questions I asked, which were: What are your areas of specialization? What framework or approach do you follow in therapy? What experience do you have with individual or couples therapy? Lesbian issues? From her answers, I knew that my opinions and feelings would be validated and supported, which is very important to me in this time of such intense self-discovery and confusion.

— JOAN

When you enter therapy, pay close attention to how well your needs are being met and whether your therapist appears to be interested and attentive to you. One woman wrote to me:

I have been seeing a straight therapist for treatment of depression. She has shared cognitive skills that continue to help me. However, since the very beginning of our work together, she has somewhat ignored my requests for insight concerning my "married life to lesbian life" journey. Recently she left me a message saying that she has been feeling professionally compromised and she needs to evaluate that.

Understandably, this woman was confused by her therapist's behavior. You always have a right to bring up questions and concerns about how your therapist is conducting the sessions. It is appropriate to tell her or him if at any time you question the benefits of the process.

An experienced therapist should listen to your concerns non-defensively and without judgment. She should take time to try to understand your feelings and be willing to examine her own methods and behavior. Most therapists recognize the value of patient feedback for honing their skills and for better understanding each patient and her specific needs. It's important to periodically evaluate how therapy feels; you, ultimately, are the judge of the efficacy of the therapy.

Talking to Friends and Family

If you're married and in conflict—unsure of where you're headed and confused about your sexuality—it can be difficult to confide in others. But if you're in free-fall and your life is unraveling, it's likely that close friends and family members will notice. If you're trying to avoid discussions that could lead to unwanted questions, it's natural that those with whom you've been close might be more distant now. As it becomes increasingly difficult to talk about most aspects of your life, you'll be faced with perhaps even daily conflict about whether to talk to them and what to say.

In high school, I had a teacher I admired, I wanted to be around her all the time. We became friends and she is still my friend today. I want to tell her what I'm going through, but I'm afraid she will start questioning my feelings for her, now and in the past. We have never discussed our views on gays/lesbians, so I'm not sure how she feels about it. I have shared so much with her and she helped me through some rough times, but how do I start or do I dare? I don't want to lose her in my life, but I feel I want her to know who I really am.

— BOBBI

You don't have to know you are lesbian or have a clear label for your sexuality before talking to trusted people about your current struggles. Support will be available to you only if you decide to share your circumstances with a few trusted individuals. If you feel you can't talk to anyone, you may need to work through feelings of shame before coming out to others. When the time is right, talking provides a terrific release. Some women, who are fortunate enough to experience their sexual reorientation with feelings of joy and pride, may face a different challenge. They are so blind to homophobia that when they come out to others, they are shocked if their excitement is met with a negative response. Ideally, as they move through their coming-out process, they'll understand the reality of homophobia, but won't allow themselves to be discouraged from maintaining a pride in their authentic selves. Your decision to speak to other people in your life about your love for women is affected by how you are feeling about yourself and your actions, and how close you are to self-acceptance.

> *I haven't "come out" to anyone outside of my family yet. I don't know that I will ever come out to everyone. I don't feel a great need to right now, and as long as my husband and my family live in this area, I don't want to be the cause of any more pain or embarrassment for them. They didn't choose this path, I did.*
>
> — MARTA

Marta has not resolved her feelings of guilt regarding her family. It is best for her to wait until she can speak with self-assurance about her choices before coming out to other people. Some women feel that they will always choose to be "discreet" about their sexuality. If they are able to reach a point of pride in themselves, their level of caution usually changes.

We cannot allow others to be the arbiters of our decision about when to reveal our true and authentic selves. If and when you become ready to do so, speaking the truth to significant people in your life can be empowering. Take time to decide whom you feel comfortable revealing yourself to. In the process of coming out about your exploration, you are opening the doors to greater intimacy. Ramona describes her approach:

> *I made a list of friends I wanted to tell, and, for a while, started gauging my feelings when I was with them. Did it feel like a good moment? Were we in a place where both they and I would feel comfortable with whatever reaction they were going to have? If it didn't feel "right," even if I'd told myself, "I'm going*

*to tell them tonight," I wouldn't say anything. I got comfortable
listening to my inner voice and holding off until I felt ready.*

— RAMONA

It is generally best to start disclosing your feelings with the people in your life who are most likely to be supportive. Positive reactions build confidence to continue sharing your truth with others. Ramona continued:

*I was very worried about coming out to both friends and family.
I didn't want to lose those I love. But I got to a point where I needed to
tell them all —I needed it for ME. When I came to the conclusion that I
couldn't control how they would react, I found some peace, knowing I was
doing what would make me most comfortable . . . being honest with them
about who I am and how great it felt to have accepted that part of me.*

Veronica had to overcome years of being a caretaker and trying to make other people happy before she talked to others. By the time she came out to her family, she almost didn't care how they responded. She focused on taking care of herself. In her words:

*There will always be people who reject me and always people who
accept me. Having supportive, positive reactions from friends has been
incredible as I start coming out to people. There have been some negative ones, too, but I just have to remember that **I am not responsible
for others' emotions.***

After working hard to develop self-acceptance, Kari decided that the friends and family who loved her would want her to be happy. She recognized the importance of communicating her happiness to the people she chose to tell. Coming out to other people is an act of love, a decision to bring these people closer to you so that they can understand and share your joy. Kari shared her coming out process with chosen friends:

I decided I would start the conversation with very positive wording, like, "You are one of my best friends. I care for you very much, and I want to share something with you that makes me very happy. I'm a lesbian." I am convinced that my positive feelings about finally being able to be all of ME with them made it easier for them to accept the news. They saw me happily sharing this news with them, and they recognized they didn't have to worry about me. Well, there is no turning back now. I finally told one of my very good friends about my past relationship with a woman. She was VERY supportive. I feel sooooo much better just having talked about it to someone other than my therapist. Wow, I feel so liberated!

Coming out to others is a life-long process. You will always need to take care in deciding with whom to reveal yourself. Over time, however, coming out to others becomes a decision, just one of many, about how much information you share in any given conversation. If you've hidden your feelings for women for a long time, you may have developed a habit of rarely talking about yourself or your personal life. I remember a time when I worked in a very liberal women's agency shortly after leaving my marriage. The staff often gathered and talked about their husbands and their weekend activities. I didn't join in; I felt I was just a more private person. The day came when a new woman was hired who was an out lesbian. I noticed she joined in the chatty conversations, adding news about her life with her partner. It was an important awakening moment for me. Being private was the way

I handled my discomfort about coming out to others. I gradually became more open, and consequently, more intimate with many of the people in my life as I overcame my fears about revealing my sexual orientation.

WHAT YOU CAN DO NOW

Remind yourself: Action will initiate change and usually is necessary in order to break out of depression. Act now to develop new resources.

Ask yourself this question: What fears currently stand in the way of my talking to someone new about my current situation? What are my fears about contacting any new resource?

Practice this technique for handling difficult feelings: A common defense most of us have at times is offering yourself reasons why you can't do something even before you try. Make a list of the ways you tell yourself "Yes, but…" For example, "I want to go to a gay bookstore, but someone might recognize me if I go." Don't censor yourself; make the list as long as you can. Next, change your statement into "Yes, and . . ." such as "Yes, and here are the obstacles I must overcome to accomplish this." Or "Yes, and here is a list of steps I must take to do this."

Take one step: Contact one new resource, whether it is a person you know or one of the resources suggested in this book.

CHAPTER 10

DECISION-MAKING AS A DEVELOPMENTAL PROCESS

In my experience, you have to embrace the pain, feel it, then move on in your own time. Then, hopefully, the joy will emerge and some kind of peace will prevail.

— MIDGE

Overview of the Decision-Making Process

If you are a married woman, you carry the burden of making choices that directly affect the very people who depend on you for love and a feeling of safety. The path you choose alters your family's path as well. When you are flooded with questions about past, present and future decisions, it's extremely difficult to put things into perspective. At the beginning, you are searching for answers that may seem elusive. Even if you're someone who is normally self-assured and decisive, it's often the case at this juncture to feel ambivalent or as if you're floundering. Today you might want to work on your marriage; tomorrow you can't let go of your girlfriend and are adamant about leaving your husband. Ask Joanne internet readers often ask, "Is what I'm feeling normal?" Usually it is the women who have made some clear decisions who can reassure others that it's all normal.

The past three years I haven't even had one foot out the door or one foot in the door. I feel like I've been spinning in the revolving door. I'm so grateful this has stopped! Now it's just a matter of fully stepping out! I'm still anticipating taking a little time making that step.

—ROSEMARY

Throughout my struggle, I felt that if I could resolve these problems, I would be prepared to handle any challenge in life. Each married woman faces many critical questions. Here is perhaps the most daunting question: Is it possible to reconcile the experience of loving women, romantically and/or sexually, with a commitment to a heterosexual marriage? What follows are some thoughts to keep in mind as you seek the answers most appropriate for you.

Early Decisions Often Change

Most decisions are not final. Sometimes the decision to take action is important mainly for the purpose of learning. You won't know what you are capable of until you try. When I began to imagine "being" with a woman, I reached out to the one lesbian friend I was getting to know. We had a discussion about sexual identity. At that time, I thought that bisexuality was a panacea; bisexuals, I believed, had the best of both the lesbian and straight world. I didn't understand why my friend laughed at that idea. Later, when she and I became lovers, I learned that being involved with two people was far more complicated than I had imagined. The guilt and ensuing chaos was not part of the fantasy.

When Stuck, Take Action

Action can be something as simple as buying a book. Or it may be more life-altering, such as joining a support group or calling a therapist. Feeling stuck often provides the impetus to taking action. The outcome sometimes feels right and sometimes feels disastrous. If you take action and things don't work out the way you thought they would, try to avoid interpreting the result as a sign of failure. Every new piece of information will help to resolve your areas of conflict. You may decide, for example, to break off all contact with a lover in order to commit serious effort to your marriage. After a few days, you decide that it's imperative for you talk with her. Or she leaves you a message and you decide to return the call. The contact resumes. There is something to learn in these experiences. Perhaps you were not ready for a complete cut-off, or the decision was not something you are fully convinced is right.

Evaluate Each Action

Heighten your awareness of what you are doing every step of the way. The creative exploration that you are undertaking may feel risky and may stretch you in ways that seem foreign to you. Keep track of your feelings as you enter this new territory. Be thoughtful and patient. If you take the time to evaluate your actions, each new venture will add to your self-awareness.

It wasn't always easy moving forward and I second-guessed myself with regularity. But I kept asking myself if, knowing what I know now about myself, I can blend back into my heterosexual marriage. . . and ignore who I am. The answer . . . "no." So I inched

*forward a little more. And second-guessed myself again. One day
I realized I had moved enough inches that I was on the other side.*

—NAN

Discomfort Can Push You Toward Impulsive Decision-Making

Many women feel so uncomfortable that, in trying to assuage their
guilt or fear, they end up acting impulsively. Be gentle with yourself and
just consider these quick-fix attempts a form of trial and error. What follows is an example of one woman's need for a quick-fix solution.

*I told my husband about my feelings for women. What a mess it
has been. I couldn't handle living with him, so I ended up moving out. My husband and I aren't officially divorced yet, and I
feel like I'm cheating on him. I know I should break things off
with my girlfriend, but I have strong feelings for her. I'm in way
over my head and feel like I'm drowning.*

— CANDY

Effective Decision-Making Is a Process

Decisions that feel right and acceptable generally come after
long contemplation and negotiation of the entire decision-making
process. The information that results from any action will help you
to make substantiated, thoughtful decisions for the future. While
you are intellectually evaluating the information you gather, you are
paying attention to your feelings and responses, as well. You may
find that as you try to make changes, old habits emerge that drag
you back toward what's familiar, and often, more comfortable.

I battled with myself for eight months about whether to stay
married or to explore my attractions further. The ambivalence and

unhappiness was more than I could tolerate. So I made a decision and told my therapist that I wanted to separate from my husband. He began to explore with me in detail how I might envision the separation. The further I went into the scenario, the more distraught I became. I realized then that I couldn't do it. It was another three months before I felt ready. Part of my preparation involved discarding preconceived ideas about divorce and my fears about how other people would judge me.

Question Your Beliefs

We all have beliefs that need to be questioned as we grow and change over our lifetimes. Our belief systems become more complex as we develop our critical thinking abilities. You may end up rejecting some views, such as religious beliefs. Rosalie ended up in terrible conflict over her religious views:

I have been a Bible-believing Christian woman for the past twelve years. My life has been the church. Right now I am reconciled with my husband even though I want to pursue being with a woman. I feel that I need to stay in the marriage because it is right and because of my Christian background.

— ROSALIE

Your opinions about gay and lesbian lifestyles, about the effects of divorce, and about the importance of personal happiness all may need to be scrutinized. Reading, talking to knowledgeable people, and using your powers of observation will help you to reassess your beliefs. Only you can determine which values you want to live by. In one instance, Micki changed her belief system, and she found peace.

I thought keeping my family under the same roof while loving another woman was "keeping a healthy, unbroken home." The family looked good on the outside, but the people within the home were falling apart. An unbroken home is much more than a group of people living together under the same roof. Now my children are at peace and my ex-husband no longer feels the pain of my indecision. He is finding a wonderful life for himself. We now can come together and feel a peace that was so missing. My advice is not to look at the physical form in which you live, but at the emotional one.

— MICKI

How to Confront Your Beliefs

You can change your life by altering your attitude. Negative self-talk can often lead to depression or to feelings of self-hatred. The messages we tell ourselves are usually unconscious, so part of the work of improving our lives is to become aware of our internal dialogue. There are specific methods developed in the field of cognitive therapy by authors such as David Burns, M.D. that will help you identify and confront beliefs that lead to self-recrimination. Below are some examples of damaging beliefs that were stated in messages from women online:

- *I am such an awful person for thinking I might be gay or bisexual.*
- *I've always tried to do the right thing. My mother tells me that the Bible says "it" is wrong. I feel so guilty.*
- *I do not want to be gay. It is not an easy life; society does not treat you well.*

When you develop a habit of seeking authentic positive messages even in the midst of troubled times, positive feelings will follow. It is possible to use specific techniques to overcome negative feelings by confronting your thoughts. Observe how each of the following assessment methods could change the following statement:

Being gay is not an easy life; society does not treat you well.

1. **List all of the possible ways the statement distorts the truth.** There are parts of society that accept gays and lesbians. You have some choice about when and where to reveal your lifestyle.
2. **Examine the evidence. What are the facts? Are you discounting positive information?** If you know any lesbians well enough, speak to them about their experience.. You will likely find that there are both advantages and disadvantages to their lifestyle. While there have been significant changes in recent years, there is still homophobia in our culture. However, most women feel relief about becoming authentic and are more at peace with themselves when they accept their sexuality. Self-acceptance fosters a sense of pride and integrity.
3. **Are you jumping to conclusions?** The news media often highlights the problem areas. You may find more support than you are expecting. We often imagine the worst-case scenarios when we are afraid. Are you assuming that your family or close friends will never accept you? This may not be true.
4. **Are you holding a double standard? Would you think this way about a friend in the same situation?** If your friend thought she was lesbian, would you reject her? Would you encourage her to change because of some other people's attitudes? Is it possible your close friends would, above all, want you to be happy?

5. Talk to other people; do they all think the same way?
Contact an assortment of people whom you trust. If possible, include both gay and straight people.

For instance, online Leanna confronts the notion that "being gay is not an easy life":

There is nothing that compares to the feeling of being who you really are. The peacefulness that will eventually settle in your soul is worth every bump in the road.

6. How will this attitude help or hurt you? Is there a more positive way to look at the situation? When you approach people with fear or express a sense of shame, they are less likely to feel that being gay is a positive alternative life. If you were to think, "It is my right to love whom I choose," or "I am a good, loving person," other people may well respond to you more positively. If it's hard for you to sincerely feel these positive perspectives, it may help to work on these areas. A gay-friendly professional may help you to undo some old habits of believing you are unworthy of the same freedoms and happiness afforded others. Below is an online comment from one woman about being gay:

When I feel sorry for myself, I think about my love for a woman (although unrequited) and I imagine what life would be like with NEVER having those feelings for another person— so I am fortunate really, aren't I?

7. Are you thinking only in black-and-white terms; do you allow for shades of gray? We tend to be less fearful when we avoid all-or-nothing expectations. For example, some of your life may be more difficult and some of it will be easier. Your parents may not accept you initially, but with time, they may adjust. It is possible they may never like your choice but will still love you and hope for your happiness.

Journaling to Facilitate Decision-Making

Use your journal to write about some of the beliefs that cause you pain. One way to get in touch with these unconscious beliefs is to recall recent events that upset you. Can you identify the thoughts that were behind your negative responses? Write down each thought as a simple statement. Then,confront each statement using the above techniques. This exercise tends to promote more flexible thinking and will help you feel more optimistic.

Below are examples of two women who grew up with the belief that leaving a marriage was an act of selfishness. As they reexamine and confront those beliefs, they are able to see their decisions in a positive, nonjudgmental light.

My ex-husband and I had many talks about what he deserved. We talked about how our children deserved parents who were true to themselves and not "following the rules." I know as a child, I was able to sense happy parents from sad ones.

I left behind a beautiful home, unlimited shopping, few work hours, and the freedom to travel four times a year to five-star hotels. Staying was materialistic, staying was selfish; the hard thing to do was to let go of the easy life and live out my true nature.

Childhood Experiences Form Many Beliefs

A common area of disagreement and often a great source of pain is how loved ones, especially children, will be affected by divorce. On the Internet, women who themselves are the children of divorce have shared their experiences. as Such discussions emphasize how our childhood experiences influence the messages we internalize and transmit to our children. Observe how different the following women's attitudes are, based on their personal experiences of divorce.

I am a child of divorce and I have never recovered. I have all kinds of love and abandonment issues because of it. I would never forgive myself for destroying my children's lives.

— ELLA

I am also a child of divorce. I have no issues or negative feelings about divorce at all. Divorced parents can be just as involved and often MORE involved in their children's lives as married couples. It's all up to the parents. I have known people who have used their beliefs to convince children that the divorce will completely destroy their lives, and of course it does. A self-fulfilling prophecy . . .

— LATISHA

Self-sacrificing on my mother's part left me with severe issues in my adult relationships, from fear of intimacy to involving myself in numerous unavailable relationships. A less-than-ideal marriage became a tomb for my parents as the years wore on, and it slowly took its toll on all of us in the family.

— MERRY

It is extremely important to look into your own experiences of family and childhood successes and difficulties to understand the roots of your belief systems. Keep yourself open to learning about other perspectives. If your childhood was painful because of the way your parents handled a situation, ask yourself whether you might be able to handle a similar circumstance better ... with some guidance. Maintaining a positive outlook helps to mold your reality. A few years ago, I was amused to hear one of my adult daughters describing her childhood as so much more "normal" than that of most of her friends. She was not only a child of divorce, but of a lesbian mother. Why did she feel so normal? Perhaps because the problems that arose during her childhood were not viewed as catastrophes. Or because she didn't feel conflict or negativity from her father or me regarding my sexuality and lifestyle.

What I have learned is that we must examine and work on our own perspectives in order to affect our most powerful form of communication, modeling through our own behavior. If you view divorce or coming out as lesbian as a crisis, it is likely your children will view it the same way. You can provide them a very different lesson: change may not be easy, but is sometimes necessary to find eventual fulfillment and happiness.

Setting Priorities: A Path to Letting Go

Prioritizing is essentially deciding that one thing is more important than another. As we mature, our priorities naturally evolve, but changing circumstances can have a profound effect on priorities, reordering them in ways you might earlier have thought to be impossible.

What is most important to me? Being close to my family? Being with someone I feel passion for? Having children (although I know it's best not to get pregnant at this time)? Can I be true to myself and go back to my husband?

— BECKY

Becky faces the difficult task of establishing priorities. She knows a number of things that are important to her, but her desires conflict. Challenging moral questions arise when you must decide which of a variety of personal values should come first. When you feel stuck, ask yourself: Where have I placed myself in my order of priorities? Where do I draw the line? Which of my values am I unwilling to compromise? What is the one thing I will not relinquish? And then we all must also be aware that we may well have to make difficult choices: setting your priorities can sometimes be a painful reminder of what we have to let go of.

What got me into my mess was trying to "have it all." I wanted to be with my girlfriend, keep the marriage, keep the house and friends, and keep going on my journey of self-discovery. These are very conflicting paths and goals. I couldn't be all things to all people and be true to me.

— MARLA

Often when we want to "have it all," as Marla says above, we are trying to avoid the necessity of making priorities and choices. For Marla, it turned out that "having it all" meant she wasn't fully experiencing anything. Your decisions may require you to let go of not only material things but often more abstract concepts: old beliefs, dreams of your future, aspects of your old identity. During my exploration, after months of miserable paralysis, I realized that I had been unable to let go of my dreams for the future. I had always imagined growing old with my husband, watching our children grow up together, living a comfortable life, and working out our differences. When I realized that most of my remorse was associated with the future, it became easier to imagine letting go of what was actually happening in the present.

It's natural to try to hold on to the familiar. Even a marriage that has been unhappy offers comfort in its familiarity. Lila, an online correspondent, described her marriage as mostly cold and distant, punctuated by occasional angry outbursts from her husband. She dealt with her unhappiness by having occasional affairs with women. Over time, her self-esteem diminished, until she wasn't sure she was capable of a better life with a woman, even though she realized she was lesbian.

Lila couldn't let go. Any time she began to think seriously about separating from her husband, she returned to old thoughts that he wasn't such a bad person and perhaps she just hadn't tried hard enough. When she and her husband kept their distance, avoiding arguments, Lila could tolerate the marriage. But her attractions never went away. The longer she held on, the more she felt angry with herself for her indiscretions and inability to change the status quo. Eventually her husband decided to leave.

You may believe you know where you want your life to go, but you can't seem to take the steps to get there. If you have been stuck in a holding pattern for years, the way Lila was, take time to explore your resistance to letting go. This type of self-examination is best done with the help of a professional because the patterns that keep you stuck are often unconscious and difficult to identify.

Decision-Making Can Be an Impetus to Transformation

Rarely is the chosen path clear of obstacles. What changes need to take place in your external and internal world in order to make the transition? Some of those changes may have little to do with your sexuality or your marriage. Sylvie writes:

I know I must leave my marriage to be clear to move ahead, but there are two issues that hold me back. One is my employability, having been out of the market for about ten years; the other is that I am a recluse and an introvert. I have NO close friends of my own, so I have no support system other than the lesbian therapist I have seen briefly.

Whether you plan to leave your husband or to work on the marriage, you will likely discover during your exploration that there are aspects of yourself that are underdeveloped. Sylvie recognizes that she will have a hard time meeting new people if she continues to isolate herself. She needs to develop both skills and courage to overcome her shyness. Fortunately, most women discover that they have more internal resources to draw upon than they might have expected. For all of us, the energy we have been expending to block our authenticity can instead become available for our transformation. No doubt you've marshaled your skills at other turning points in your life. When you can no longer rely on your spouse, you may be motivated to access and develop these abilities.

We have all ventured into new territory in our lives before, wondering how it was going to be. Granted, THIS is huge, but when we first went away to college, or first moved in with someone, or first got married, moved to a new town, all new and unknown, we found our internal strengths to manage.

— **FAITH**

In my own life, my husband was more extraverted than I was, and I found comfort in his ability when we were socializing. When I discovered that most women are somewhat shy about approaching other women, I attempted to push past my shyness. I realized it might take forever if I waited to be approached by a woman. In a heterosexual culture, most women aren't taught the art of courting; this has been traditionally a man's domain. For women like Sylvie, there are books on overcoming shyness and on how to meet women, and a women's therapy or support group will help for social skill development. When facing divorce, most women are at a disadvantage financially. If you stayed at home to take care of the kids, you may be able to get financial help from your husband for the time you devoted to handling the childcare. This was part of the final agreement between my husband and me. He had advanced his career while I was taking primary care of the kids when they were young. We took this into account when making our divorce settlement. Contact a lawyer to learn about your rights. If life with your husband is peaceful, you may prefer to stay together while you go back to school or search for the right job.

Women whose work was in the home may need to update their skills or develop new ones to reenter the job market. I separated from my husband just before I returned to school to get my graduate degree in social work. I learned that when you are determined to move forward, you often find creative ways to manage the changes that must take place for both you and your spouse. Our custody and financial agreements took into account both of our particular schedules. We took into consideration the time that I needed to reach a point of financial self-sufficiency. During major life transitions, people are especially open to self-examination. Take this opportunity to discover what aspects of yourself you want to change or develop. In her message, Mel reveals a common theme for women: a sense of losing herself over the course of marriage. As Mel takes steps toward being true to herself, she is recapturing her vitality.

Expand my LIFE!!! Grow and live. My eyes are open. When did I lose myself? Now to find myself again. These last couple of weeks have been enlightening. I see the leaves on the trees. The sunsets are more brightly hued. Music is sweeter. I feel so alive.

Any relationship you develop at this point, whether with your husband or with a woman, will benefit from this kind of assessment. Do you want to become more assertive, be more affectionate, manage your own finances? Like many other women, I had to learn to handle my own finances after my separation. It wasn't easy at first, but I felt a real sense of mastery as I learned these new skills. Taking charge of areas you have never handled before is part of taking control of your life.

I signed my lease today. Will get the new keys to my apartment tomorrow. After fifteen good, not great, years of marriage, I'm leaving to authenticate my life. For me, the greatest emotional hurdle was recognizing that I could make it on my own. Just viewing apartments, scummy versus livable (affordable) allowed me to say—okay—I can do this. It's going to be all right.

— HILLARY

You may discover, after clarifying your desire to be with a woman, that you still have unresolved intimacy issues. Some relationship problems have little to do with the gender of the person you are with. Regardless of feeling "in love," some women observe a continuing need to push their girlfriends away whenever they begin to get close. Other women recognize a pattern of falling in love with straight or unavailable women. This time of upheaval is often a great motivator to address old problems and to make significant changes.

I learned something important about myself when I realized I had found a love that was unavailable and unwilling to get involved. I had my own personal fear of allowing love to be available in my life; there are painful issues I need to heal within myself before a fulfilling relationship will enter my life.

— MARISOL

Life becomes more joyful and more meaningful as you develop increasing authenticity. Turning points that are shadowed by suffering create motivation to get to know yourself. Becoming more authentic goes beyond finding a name for your sexual orientation; it reaches into all aspects of life. You may feel more open and comfortable with other people once you acknowledge your truths. I developed closer friendships after acknowledging my sexuality. Women often talk about a change in their ability to parent. Increased happiness helps them to enjoy, to focus, and be available for their children.

I am a better Mom since acknowledging myself (in a thousand different ways). Not sick, depressed, unmotivated, controlling, or sheepish anymore.

— NAOMI

I was afraid that I would have regrets when I moved out of my marital home, but at first all I felt was the joy of liberation. I had moved into a modest apartment with a colleague of mine and another roommate. When one of the women made dinner for me that first night, I realized I hadn't had a meal cooked for me at home since I was married. I reveled in the experience of freedom. Most of my grieving had occurred before I left the marriage. It would recur periodically when my husband and I had to work out new details for the children, for holidays and events, and when the divorce was final.

Throughout the first months, I felt that I had left an entire way of life. In the beginning, the children lived with my husband on weekdays while I was going to graduate school. During this period, my daughters picked up the chicken pox, then the measles and numerous colds, and then one of them broke her wrist on the playground at school. I got the message. It was time to get back to parenting. I began to reenter the family world with a new feeling of joy and renewed energy and love for my children.

The following excerpts express the empowerment women feel when they finally get comfortable with their new sense of self:

I don't fit in the lesbian world or the heterosexual world, so I decided to just LIVE in the world. I must accept that who ever I decide to commit to next must know about my bisexuality, the struggles I have had in the past, yet believe I am a "normal" partner for them now. For me, there is no "right" sex, just the "right" partner.

Authenticate your life! is my new mantra. Doesn't mean I have to label myself, just means I have to do what will give my life meaning and balance. So I can be the best of who I am for everyone. I know who I am.

For years I hated myself because of my sexuality. I could only describe it as a torment. But eventually I started to think if I could believe in myself and accept and love myself, the torment would fade, and it has, and it continues to fade.

WHAT YOU CAN DO NOW

Remind yourself: We all have the capacity to be courageous, to take a stand, when we break from the norm to think for ourselves.

Ask yourself this question: What beliefs, feelings, or things do I need to let go of (such as outdated beliefs, dreams of a particular future, knowing how life could be with a woman, economic security, having everyone's approval)? Write about this in your journal.

Practice this technique for handling feelings: For every fear or negative belief you have about yourself, make a statement that expresses just the opposite. Turn this into a list of positive affirmations and keep them readily accessible for the times you feel uncertain or fearful. For example, if you say to yourself, "I won't be able to support myself," instead say, "I will do what I need to do to learn how to support myself." Or if you say, "I am afraid of being viewed as different or an outsider because of being gay," instead say, "I will become comfortable and proud of who I am and others will respond positively."

Take one step: Write a brief essay in your journal about how far you have come on your personal journey. Focus on all of the positive changes that you have made. This exercise is not about what remains to be done but an acknowledgement of your accomplishments. These may include attitude changes or the steps you have taken, regardless of how large or small.

CHAPTER 11

ASK JOANNE

Questions from Readers

It breaks my heart and comforts me at the same time to have discovered the "Ask Joanne" internet site, and I must admit it has had a profound impact on me. The reality of married women loving women and being true to themselves can come with such suffering, confusion, and loss that the struggle will always be burned indelibly in my heart. The idea that you, Joanne, are here to provide this forum with your wisdom, guidance and life lessons is deserving of a standing ovation.

—"ASK JOANNE" ONLINE MEMBER

When I first began writing *Living Two Lives* in 2003, my internet Q & A site, "Ask Joanne" (www.askjoanne.net), was small enough for me to answer every question posed by the married women who were seeking help from me. Today, this online community has expanded to over 1,000 women and I'm unable to provide the same role. I'm so pleased to see that many of the women, at different stages of transition, have stepped up to offer each other guidance and support. For many women, this community has been a lifeline during a time of uncertainty and turmoil.

This chapter is set up in a question and answer format, modeled on the Q & A section of the "Ask Joanne" online discussion board. You'll find discussion here of an array of issues that women have brought to me, which include some of their worst fears: negative responses from spouses, fear or guilt about coming out, hurting the kids, being "too old," or being unable to find a partner; feeling unable to move forward with a decision; and myths about lesbian relationships. In every instance, I offer a positive perspective to help you move through your transition with strength and courage.

Some of the questions in this chapter relate to the same issues from the first edition of *Living Two Lives,* but will expand the discussion. My "Ask Joanne" online message board now has a specific forum for concerns about coming out and about life after coming out. These forums and this chapter include topics about lesbian relationships and stepfamily issues.

Catastrophe or Opportunity?

I've been married for twenty-two years to a husband who is a good man, but I've known for many years that I don't love him the way a wife should. My life isn't bad; it's just not happy. I'm in such conflict: sometimes I feel like I'm doing irreparable harm to my family and other times I feel like my urgency to change my life overrides everybody else's needs. My parents are pushing me to save my marriage. Am I selfishly destroying the lives of my loved ones? Can I really start my life over and drag my husband and children into something they didn't ask for or expect?

For all of us, when the bedrock certainties of our lives, our most solid and reliable beliefs and thoughts, begin to shift, we may find ourselves in crisis. Like me, you may have thought at the time you married that you were reliably heterosexual, a person capable of commitment, perhaps faithful and honest. Your beliefs may have differed from mine, but you probably felt as certain as I did about the qualities and attributes that made you who you are. And then it happens—we're blindsided by a new experience or a sudden aware-ness, and we begin to question our core beliefs, not just about our-selves, but about our past or future. For instance, many women who begin questioning their sexual orientation end up re-examining the religious teachings of their childhood, teachings that provided their spiritual foundation. They suddenly recognize that their religion would not accept them if they were openly gay. Or, like many mar-ried women, you may have believed you would have a long stable family life with your husband and children. At this juncture in life, you are wondering whether your husband can give you what you need for genuine happiness, or whether you can offer him the same. The dream of growing old together now seems uncertain.

Your confusion and worry about the future may correspond to the feeling of alienation from self—how can you trust emotions and behaviors so new to you? In 1977 when I fell in love with a woman, had an extramarital affair, lied about it, and broke my marriage vows, I was a stranger to myself. My self-identity was derailed and I didn't like what I saw. This behavior made me uncomfortable and I needed to find a way to make sense of it. In hindsight, I realize that some hidden part of myself was calling for attention. Married women who discover their attraction to women are usually in crisis until they find a way to reconcile their two different experiences of love—for a man or for a woman. You are facing decisions that bear enormous consequences. Your normal ways of resolving problems may prove insufficient. I've learned at such times to look for guidance in the lessons of great spiritual teachers. When reason isn't enough, certain spiritual teachings often help us unravel the mysteries of the human spirit in a way that encourages us to rise above our adversities.

Many women in your situation feel they are falling apart when they begin to question the viability of their marriage. You are facing a transformational moment. One reader describes the chaotic feelings that led her to a sense of paralysis:

> I'm consumed with sadness, doubt, uncertainty, lack of feeling, too much feeling—clear feelings of love and a decision to go back to my husband, and then clear and poignant feelings of love and a desire to go with my girlfriend. I want to fix everything with him and have it be back to where it was, only better . . . yet I cannot leave her.

The despair of your crisis may become the motivation you need to face the questions that rise to the surface. Elizabeth Lesser, a spiritually-oriented writer, shares stories of people who have faced serious life-changing events in her book, *Broken Open*. The people she writes about developed a quality of unusual openness during their time of turmoil. While the life events could have been catastrophic, they instead became a vehicle for new insights and behaviors that changed these individuals' lives in wonderful and dramatic ways.

In my own life, during times when I feel most vulnerable, I tend to reveal myself more openly to the people close to me. I often ask for help and am usually more receptive to others' thoughts and perspectives. During the period of transition in my marriage, I realized that in spite of the deep suffering I had experienced, I wouldn't exchange it for the numbness I had lived with up to that time. I promised myself to stay alert to all of life and to *feel* all that life had to offer. In the recent experience of facing my partner's death, I've learned that the vulnerability and openness brought on by this crisis has brought me closer in very meaningful ways to the people in my life.

Broken Open presents some of Lesser's life changes and the particular ways in which she found a path to rekindle the joys of life. She describes a journey, which she calls the Phoenix Process, in which one descends into despair and then emerges into one's true self and inner peace. Her Phoenix Process suggests the value of searching for the seeds of renewal that are generally hidden in most of our terribly painful times. She describes the Phoenix Process in the following passage:

"You and I are the Phoenix. Our lives ask us to die and to be reborn every time we confront change—change within ourselves and change in our world . . . . When there is nothing left to lose, we find the true self—the self that is whole, the self that is enough, the self that no longer looks to others for definition, or completion, or anything but companionship on the journey . . .

We all experience change and loss throughout our lives—through big and dramatic life-quakes and in smaller, more habitual ways. It takes work to use crisis and stress as vehicles for transformation . . . .The Phoenix Process is a journey that is different for everyone, and therefore it is a trek into uncharted territory. It is erroneous, and even unhelpful, to compare one person's journey with another's—all are different, and one is not more profound or important than another…It's all in the way we approach the changing nature of life; it's all in the courage to say yes to whatever comes our way; it's in the way we listen for the messages in the flames and dig for the treasure in the ashes.

Each one of us, regardless of our situation, is looking for the same treasure in the ashes. We are in search of our most authentic, vital, generous, and wise self. What stands between that self and us is what burns in the fire. Our illusions, our rigidity, our fear, our blame, our lack of faith, and our sense of separation: all of these—in varying strengths and combinations—are what must die in order for a more true self to arise. If we want to turn a painful event into a Phoenix Process, we must name what needs to burn within us. . . . Some people realize what must burn in the fire is their fear—fear of their own power, fear of change, fear of loss, fear of others. Some people name an inability to feel, a crippling cynicism, a sense of shame, a stance of anger."

— LESSER, ELIZABETH.
BROKEN OPEN: HOW DIFFICULT TIMES CAN HELP US GROW

Lesser's stories about herself and other people she has known who survived what seemed like insurmountable challenges are the kind of vehicle I have found helpful during my lonely, uncertain times. When I felt frightened by the prospect of possibly leaving my husband and becoming self-sufficient, I discovered the importance of bearing witness to other people's journeys. I asked every woman I met who seemed to have "come out" through some kind of adversity to tell me her story. In doing so, I gathered courage for myself to come out while married. Years later, I wondered how observing the struggle of my partner's grueling cancer treatment could possibly offer me something positive. The experience taught me about my capacity for nurturing Judy and staying by her side throughout her ordeal, even when her pain was hard to witness. I did things I wouldn't have thought I could do. I also found ways to ask for help, which often wasn't easy, and in the process created more intimate relationships with my friends. With each crisis and each loss, I've developed a stronger faith in the value of patiently looking for the treasures that are hidden in times of darkness. "Patience" is the key word here. It isn't always apparent what the lessons are, but when you take time to sift through the ashes, you will probably find something worth holding close.

Fantasy or Reality?

I've been living two lives for the past year. My husband works long hours and I do most of the home care. I find time to be with my girlfriend when he comes home late or during the daytime when he is working. Life with my husband includes the real obligations of daily life. I know how wonderful I feel when I'm with my girlfriend . . . and then I go home to a good husband and my kids. I ask myself, "Self . . . which one is real? The stuff I think about all the time or the stuff that I live every day?"

I could have written these very words at the start of my own love story. When I fell in love with a woman and was still married, my thoughts of a life change seemed to fall into the realm of dreaming about the impossible. Building my life with a woman, raising my kids with a woman, "becoming" a lesbian, were all pure fantasy. With a lot of self-examination, therapy, and problem-solving, I eventually discovered that fantasy can become reality. And why not? Here's how Rachel Naomi Remen describes it in *Kitchen Table Wisdom*.

"Sometimes all that is needed is a sense of possibility. Not long ago I was walking in the rain in the place where I was born, New York City, thinking of the green place where I now live, grateful for the ease with which things grow there. Not all things grow easy. The rain made me intensely aware of the hardness and grayness of this world of cement and brick. For miles and miles there seemed to be nothing living that could respond to the rain. But the rain comes anyway. The possibility of growth is there even in the hardest times."

Opening up to possibility is what keeps us living life fully. Without dreams we humans often fall into hopelessness and depression. A wise teacher in my graduate school taught a lesson I've always remembered. As a family therapist, he had worked with a depressed young African American boy and his mother, who lived in extreme poverty in a local housing project. The therapist asked the boy about his dreams for the future. His reality was bleak; scarcity and deprivation were his norm. He was surrounded by violence and drug abuse. When asked about his dreams, the boy had none. The therapist spent most of their sessions tapping into the child's imagination, helping him to fantasize about his future. With dreams come possibilities. They may or may not come to fruition, but without them there is no chance.

You are facing a situation which may seem to be insoluble to you right now, so it's the perfect time to look for a new perspective. You might consider taking your dreams and fantasies quite seriously. Make sure the dream is about and for you, not about changing someone else. While it is possible to make changes in yourself, your choices, and your behavior, you can't do that for another person. You may not know the steps needed to reach your vision at this time, but your dreams often contain nuggets of gold. They bypass your fears and usually come from the heart.

Seeing my dreams as mere fantasies allowed me to escape the hard work required to confront the possibility of unraveling my familiar, comfortable life. It wasn't until I unexpectedly fell in love that I could tap into my yearning to live my life with a woman. At first, my dream was to have "the best of both worlds," to stay married and have an ongoing relationship with my girlfriend. It wasn't long before I realized that this early dream required that two other people—my husband and my girlfriend—wanted the same thing, too. But neither of them did.

Your dreams may be similar or quite different from my example. Too often we create a story about the perfect life, and then work it through in our minds to the point that we decide it's completely impossible. And so we never even try. While you haven't had the stresses of everyday life when you are with your girlfriend, you may have an idea of how your girlfriend handles stress, yours and hers. Any new relationship takes work to develop patterns of listening, compromising and establishing routines together. When two people want something badly, they often find ways to get there. One of the "Ask Joanne" readers describes the importance of perspective and changing her expectations.

Ha! Where there is a will there is a way—and if this is my only route to freedom right now—then I'm taking it—'cause I'm not living this way a single minute more. I'm not starting with much at all. The way I look at it there is nowhere else to go but UP!! Okay, so I thought it would be a bit different looking from my late twenties—like a big house, a big yacht to take me south (with a personal crew no less), and a lovely winter home on the beach and lots of grandkids by now. Alas, to think I stayed as long as I did to be sure that he would be okay. My advice to you ladies is that if you set your sights a little lower, then you can get out sooner. Anything is possible and we can live with almost any level of sacrifice.

This reader worked hard to let go of her beliefs about what makes her happy and how her life was supposed to unfold. A bit of humor, a lot of negotiating, and even more faith in possibilities helped her to look with optimism toward her future. I hope you will find a way to hold onto your dream and try it out, taking one step at a time, making adjustments in other areas as needed. The outcome may not turn out to be all that you imagined or it may be everything and more. You won't find out unless you try.

Coming Out Without a Partner Later in Life

How can I be sixty-two years old, married for forty years, with grown children and grandchildren, and still dealing with my sexuality? When I think about all that's involved with coming out ... leaving my husband, who is sixty-six and retired, and leaving my whole life behind, it feels overwhelming. Even though I've known about my attraction to women since I was a teenager, I've never been comfortable going in that direction. I have real questions about whether it makes sense to come out without having a partner to come out for ... especially since I'm coming out later in life.

It may sound a lot easier to make such monumental decisions when there is someone you've found as a partner. Many women only begin to explore their sexuality after becoming involved with a woman. If you've spent time on the internet sites related to married women who love women, you may have noticed much of the discussion centers on these extramarital relationships. While an affair can make things more complex, if you have no special woman in your life, divorce may feel frightening. Many people in your situation feel as if there are too many unanswered questions to take such a risk. It takes a lot of courage to face your fears without an ally or a clear picture of what you are moving toward.

The companionship of an intimate relationship can seem like an ideal buffer when the life you know is falling apart, but it comes with its own challenges. For example, many women lose sight of the larger picture (the long-range effects of their decisions) when they leave their marriage to be with someone special. They often face the danger of becoming over-invested in maintaining their new relationship, which adds another level of anxiety to an already difficult situation. Without a special woman, you're in a better position to directly confront your fears with no illusion of having someone to protect you from the emotional challenges ahead. Your decisions may be less influenced by pressures from outside yourself. When women find themselves balancing two relationships (their husband and their girlfriend) they often get caught up in the ambivalent swing of trying to please each at the expense of understanding their own needs and desires.

Your question about coming out later in life on your own raises the fears that many women have. These fears usually become less overwhelming if you examine each individually. For instance, when you wonder about coming out as a single person, try to identify your underlying concerns. During my transition, I worried about many aspects of self-sufficiency. I didn't have a partner at the time I left my marriage. I worried I might not be able to support myself financially or handle many aspects of managing a home and family alone. I was afraid of being alone and lonely. If you are interested in developing relationships with women for the first time, you may need to learn about lesbian culture and the dating norms, a daunting challenge when you're on your own. It may seem easier to negotiate the new paths of life with a companion traveler.

In *Comfortable with Uncertainty*, Tibetan Buddhist teacher Pema Chodron talks about facing our fears:

"What we are talking about is getting to know fear, becoming familiar with fear, looking it right in the eye—not as a way to solve problems, but as a complete undoing of old ways of seeing, hearing, smelling, tasting, and thinking. The truth is that when we really begin to do this, we're going to be continually humbled. Fear is a natural reaction of moving closer to the truth. If we commit ourselves to staying right where we are, then our experience becomes very vivid. Things become very clear when there is nowhere to escape."

As you approach each of your fears directly, problem-solving becomes easier. Even facing the difficulties of being identified as a lesbian in a homophobic culture may feel more daunting if you are alone. If you've waited this long to explore feelings you've known for a long time, internalized homophobia may be an obstacle. Therapy is often helpful for examining issues that may be hard to identify on your own.

When I first left my marriage, I learned that being single wasn't the same as being alone. Friends, family members, or a therapist may offer the support you need to help you make changes. I discovered that I needed to call different people when I wanted to talk, and initiate plans if I wanted to do something. You may not have the support system to help you during difficult times or may feel uncomfortable asking for support.

Loneliness is frightening to most of us, and yet it is something we all face, both with a partner or spouse, sometimes in a crowd, and when we are alone. We all develop a million ways to avoid loneliness: excessive busyness, addictions, daydreaming, or staying in a bad situation that feels more secure than facing dreaded alone time. If your decisions are guided by your fear of being alone, it might be an opportune moment to work with the fear. It's difficult to make good decisions when our fear of something in the future keeps us paralyzed.

In *When Things Fall Apart: Heart Advice for Difficult Times*, Pema Chodron writes about loneliness and facing difficult feelings:

"Usually we regard loneliness as an enemy. Heartache is not something we choose to invite in. It's restless and pregnant and hot with the desire to escape and find something or someone to keep us company. When we can rest in the middle, we begin to have a nonthreatening relationship with loneliness, a relaxing and cooling loneliness that completely turns our usual fearful pattern upside down."

Your fear of being too old to make huge life changes is understandable. After all, we live in an ageist culture that emphasizes youth. I sometimes find it challenging to confront the fears and negative messages about aging that permeate our society.

However, I've observed in my own life that one's attitude about aging can be more important than actual age itself. It's almost never too late to grow and change. In fact, we're more likely to feel youthful when we continue to challenge ourselves to improve our life. The wisdom and maturity which come with life experience can be very useful in negotiating your life transition. When I look back on my coming out process, I realize that managing my fears, letting go, and laying the foundation for a new beginning require the same kind of skills, regardless of the specific circumstances.

Our minds are adept at creating worst-case scenarios. When faced with enormous change, it's not unusual to slide into a dark place of imagined stresses; the source of your anxiety may be related to your fears about living life as a lesbian. You might weigh that fear against the suffering you have endured by hiding significant aspects of your identity, keeping secrets, or living with shame about whom you love or are attracted to. When we face ourselves honestly and learn to accept and honor what we see, somehow we magically begin to project that image outward. In many cases that projection attracts warmth and openness from others. Ultimately, you are the only one who can decide whether coming out may set you free to live life more fully or whether the fears you face are too difficult to overcome.

Hurting the Kids

My three wonderful children, ranging from ages six to ten, have been the focus of my life since I stopped work to care for them. I think I would have no problem deciding to divorce and start life over with a woman if it weren't for my kids. I love being a parent and worry terribly about destroying their lives. How can I take such a risk when it would destroy our intact family?

Like most of the married mothers I've met, you face the huge responsibility of making decisions for yourself and your family that are weighted with fear and guilt. As parents, most of us work hard to protect our children from painful experiences. This goal, of course, is impossible. There isn't a person in this world who doesn't encounter disappointment and suffering as part of being human. We may want to shield our children from unnecessary pain, but when life moves in a challenging direction, we may be most effective by helping them adopt a positive attitude about change and supporting their ability to adapt. I've observed in my therapy practice that the people who seem to struggle the most over difficult decision-making are those who resist change. Life may have taught them that change or facing uncertainty is something to be feared. If you were taught this in your family of origin, you may help your children best by working on your own fears about the future.

I recall wondering whether I would upset or hurt my kids if they saw me crying or feeling sad during the most difficult times leading up to divorce. Putting on a happy face, as some of my clients have done, often blocks honest communication with your children. They usually can sense when Mom or Dad is sad or upset, and covering it up suggests that it's not okay to express these feelings. Your children don't need to know details, especially because you haven't made clear decisions yet, but you can share with them that you are unhappy and are working to find the answers to your unhappiness. If sadness turns into a more lengthy depression, then you may need help moving forward in your process of decision-making. Children benefit from observing their parent expressing feelings and also working through those feelings. When you remain stuck in your fear and sadness, it is more likely that you will convey to your children a pessimistic attitude about the future.

Your question to me is not just about your children's future, but about your own and about what you value as a mother. Letting go of my primary parenting role was one of the most painful aspects of my divorce and coming out process. I had to learn to let go of my desire to control all of the parenting, and to instead help the kids negotiate their lives with each of their new family households. It has taken me years to realize that my children faced challenges in both families. The challenges were different, but each family structure was new to them. I gave the kids all I could when they were with me and worked on letting go when they weren't. The differences in parenting styles become far more apparent when each parent is living separately. I had to let go of my desire to have their father parent in the way that I did. It turned out that my kids were very resourceful and gradually learned to adjust to the changes in their family structure.

If you deny your own happiness for the sake of your kids, you may discover that they have an uncanny sense of your sacrifice. Children learn from our behavior and often model their lives in the same way. Did you learn, as many of us did, that your happiness is less important than everyone else's? In my training as a family therapist, my gifted teacher, MaryAnn Walters, suggested that children usually benefit from observing a mother who takes care of her own needs and values happiness for herself. Such lessons train children to take responsibility for creating a happy life.

In any stepfamily arrangement, new rules evolve when new partners exert their influence and parenting dynamics change. While creating two families wasn't what I had originally wanted or expected from my marriage, I accepted with a leap of faith that the details would work out, even though at the time I couldn't envision how. Most of us are comfortable and feel more in control when we think we know how the future will look. You may believe that if you stay in your marriage, the kids won't suffer. We each need to confront that assumption directly and honestly. When parents are unhappy together, the children usually sense it. If we are unhappy but at the same time we want what's best for the children, then some change is required, although it may not involve divorce.

Letting go of past beliefs or expectations involves a degree of trust that you will handle the specific problems when they arise. What I know now is that discovering the need to let go of things, beliefs, people, or dreams, at appropriate times opened me to new life. We all need to make space for change. I eventually spent thirty-one years with my special woman, and my children were generally happy—they had their own lives and struggles, and I continue to face the process of letting go. My adult children now talk about their early difficulties they faced in the process of embracing my life choices. They grew up at a time when gay parents weren't visible in most schools. While they were comfortable with my lesbian life at home, they tried to hide our situation from their friends. Both daughters recognize how their gradual awareness and growing acceptance of diversity has made them better human beings. They learned their lessons about letting go and moving forward toward new ideas and possibilities.

When my partner, Judy, passed away in 2011, my daughter wrote about her life with Judy and me.

My mom loved an amazing woman, and she loved her back. And that love was a gift ... to my mom and Judy, but also to me and [my sister] Beth. We grew up surrounded by a love based on a profound appreciation of the other person exactly as they are. And Beth and I soaked up this lesson about how love can be. And isn't this what a parent does? Without you even realizing it, they influence you. Influence the choices you make in your own life. Without thinking about it, I have said, I want to be loved like that. I want to create a home like that.

Fears About Husbands' Responses

My husband has had periods of emotional volatility throughout our marriage. As a result of his difficulty holding a job, he has taken more responsibility at home and I have done more of the work outside our home. I've been putting off talking to my husband. I worry that he will fall into a deep depression or possibly hurt himself if he finds out that I think I'm gay. What should I do?

It's particularly painful and frightening to be unsure of your husband's ability to handle the truth. No matter how unavailable or inept he may have been in your relationship, you may still feel responsible for hurting him. Most of the women I've encountered who are on this journey care deeply about their husbands, even if they don't feel the kind of love they long to have in an intimate partnership. Usually when one spouse begins to change the rules of marriage or starts to grow in unanticipated ways, there are reverberations. New behaviors, such as becoming more independent and speaking up assertively, or having an affair, may lead to personal growth in one or both partners, but may alternatively activate dysfunctional coping mechanisms. For example, when a client of mine told her husband that she thought she was gay, he began to drink heavily. His drinking eventually led to a mental breakdown and hospitalization. Fortunately, his extreme response ultimately helped him begin to do some important internal work for the first time by facing an earlier betrayal, his childhood history of sexual abuse by a clergy member.

It's hard to maintain a balanced perspective when you're wondering whether your husband will benefit from the life changes you're considering. You've provided the primary financial and, possibly, emotional support in your relationship, so it's natural to worry about how he'll survive if you were to leave. When you begin to question your sexual identity, you inevitably end up exploring an aspect of yourself that often conflicts with the vows of marriage. This process can lead to guilt. In fact, the questionnaires completed by all participants in my Workshops for Married Women reveal that guilt is the most consistent emotional struggle they face when questioning their current lifestyle. As women socialized in our culture, it's often second nature to simply blame ourselves for everything.

Most of us tend to worry about the responses of our loved ones. Yet, it's important to evaluate your particular marriage and circumstances. If your husband is someone who might react in an extreme way to you initiating a difficult discussion with him, you are right to be concerned. Extreme reactions such as sinking into severe, intractable depression or engaging in addictive behavior are often related to past unresolved issues. Violence and irrational or angry behavior are also potential reactions. These concerns are very real, and are likely to come up at some point in the marriage, regardless of the particular catalyst. Perhaps the most extreme projected response is suicide, a way out that offers no opportunity for learning or redemption. It is an act of violence that hurts those who survive.

If you are blaming yourself for something your husband is feeling or if you believe you haven't done enough to ensure that the process goes smoothly, it may help to do a reality check. Here are some questions to ask yourself:

- *Have you been mean or unkind in your discussions? If you have, you'll feel better if you try to change that.*
- *Did you intentionally marry your husband knowing this issue would come up? Even if you had an idea that you were attracted to women, did you think you could have a satisfying relationship with your spouse at the time you married?*
- *Do you believe you deserve to be treated with respect and caring? If guilt makes you feel that you deserve to be treated badly, you are being unfair to yourself. Your husband may have the right to be angry or hurt, but those feelings don't justify disrespectful or hurtful behavior.*

When you are deciding how to talk to your husband, try to keep in mind that you probably know him better than anyone else. You know he has a history of depression, which means you may need to be extra careful about timing and how you reveal information. If he doesn't have a support system, you might suggest starting couples counseling for a while before you bring up details that will upset him. How you decide to approach difficult discussions will impact how you feel about yourself in the end. Although you can't be certain about how your husband will react, you can try to hold yourself to a standard of respect and concern when you are talking to him. The following principles are ones I have found helpful:

- *If you're deciding how and when to have a talk, trust what you know about your husband. You have a history with him and know* his attitudes, emotional stability, and what's happening in the rest of his life.

- Be sensitive to his feelings when divulging upsetting information. He may experience a range of reactions before he comes to any acceptance.
- Being kind is not equivalent to ignoring your own happiness or well-being. Allowing yourself to be held hostage to your husband's problems will lead to resentment and discord in the relationship.
- Ultimately, we can only be responsible for our own happiness.
- Your situation may trigger difficult or painful feelings in your husband (or others), but how he handles those feelings is his responsibility.

It is essential to continue to develop a level of self-awareness that builds on the tough lessons of your life. A key aspect of self-awareness lies in working to forgive yourself for what you may not have known or been able to handle differently in the past. Forgiving ourselves is not a way of condoning our wrongs, but a vital act of compassion. When we find a way to forgive ourselves, we are also offering ourselves an opportunity to commit to changing that behavior.

Reflections on Waiting

I met my single lesbian girlfriend two years ago. After becoming close friends through working together, we fell into an intensely exciting, loving relationship. We've been involved now for about a year and a half. It seems like a long time, but I haven't been able yet to ask my husband for a separation. I can't imagine my life without her, yet I'm still struggling with the idea of breaking up my family. She says she will wait *for me, but she is so unhappy with how long this is taking and I feel bad about ruining her life and possibly my husband's and my kids'. I wonder if I should let my girlfriend go so that she can be happy again.*

When two women are deeply in love, but at different stages of readiness for commitment, a dynamic frequently develops that is predictable and often toxic. Such is the case when, like you, one woman is married and is still living with her husband and the other woman is single. In the first blush of a developing extramarital relationship, waiting to be together is suffused with dreams of a shared future. As the relationship progresses, expectations begin to grow. Disappointments and insecurities begin to interfere with the pure feelings of being in love. Your girlfriend, like most single people, probably has more available time. She has no one to whom she must report or for whom she feels responsible. Naturally, her sense of intolerance grows. To the extent that she is ready for a committed relationship, it becomes more important to share events and holidays with you and to enjoy a more spontaneous involvement. Waiting has become increasingly more unpleasant. Often, the single woman is unable to call her married girlfriend at home. She waits for phone calls, for times when her married girlfriend can get away from home for the promised rendezvous.

If your single partner is assertive and aware of her own needs, she may be asking you for more. But you are still enmeshed in your primary marital relationship, so her requests begin to feel like pressure. Married women often feel guilty and defensive in response to increasing requests. While these feelings are very real and natural, you must stay clear about your own agenda. You need to move at your own natural pace.

Much is at stake when a person is deciding whether to break up a committed relationship or a family. Both individuals are often waiting for the right time—the right time to tell your husband the truth, to take any action that will upset the kids, to become self sufficient, or to come out. Your partner has to determine when her patience with you comes at her own expense . . . when there is a right time for her to say "enough!"

How do we determine when waiting is appropriate and when it becomes dysfunctional? If you are the one waiting, here are some important questions to ask yourself.

- *In my process of waiting, am I avoiding something painful that I need to address?*
- *Is my happiness with my current life fully dependent on this thing that I'm waiting for?*
- *Am I attending to my current life, or am I always focused on what the future offers me?*
- *Is this process of waiting undermining the warmth and loving aspects of the relationship?*

Making a plan involves thinking about the future and having a degree of patience for seeing it to fruition. If you are passively waiting for a goal to be achieved, you are likely waiting for someone else to take action. When you find yourself just waiting, you could be working on your own life, even when the goal seems out of your control. When you take care of yourself in the course of waiting for change, you will begin to feel stronger, more in control, and ultimately more attractive to yourself and the ones you love. Waiting is a state of mind.

If you are participating fully in life, your sense of contentment will not be future focused. Moments of happiness are to be found right now in your life as it is. If you can't find them, or if the painful times outweigh those moments, this information might provide a catalyst to change some aspect of the way you are living.

Creating a New Family After Divorce

As part of our divorce agreement, I have kept the house in which my husband and I raised our kids, now seven and eleven years old. My girlfriend and I began our relationship about a year before I left the marriage. She gave up her apartment a year after I separated and has been living here for close to a year. She and I recently have been fighting over the kids and time issues. I feel caught in the middle, between her needs and my kids' needs. She has never lived with kids and has unrealistic expectations of them. I worry about both my kids and about our relationship.

Your current struggles are common for any stepfamily arrangement, whether gay or straight. All members of the new family constellation have to adjust to many losses, to a new love relationship at the head of the family, and to the creation of new family rules and norms. Specific to your situation, you and your children also are facing your redefined sexual identity. Because your relationship began as an affair prior to ending your marriage, you may still feel remnants of the stresses involved in disengaging from the marriage. Both you and your partner may still have many emotional responses to your process of letting go of the emotional and practical connections to your ex-husband.

You might begin by looking at what losses each of you faces. Your marriage may have been wrong or not fully satisfying for you, but you have a shared history with your husband. He and you built your own family traditions, plans for the future, and approaches to parenting. Some aspects of life with your husband may be easier to leave behind than others. Many women find the dreams for the future and established family traditions are the most difficult to let go.

Your children likely are having similar adjustment challenges. They thought their mom and dad would be together and would parent together as they grew up. They may expect the same rules and family patterns they've known so far. Your kids may be jealous of your new relationship and the amount of attention and love directed to your girlfriend. They may experience the time and attention you pay to your girlfriend as a loss. If they see you and/or their father less frequently, they may miss their old life with each of you, separate and together.

Your girlfriend has to find a place for herself in this pre-existing family unit of mom and kids. She, too, may miss the full attention she received when you would meet alone, without the kids or other distractions. Now she is required to share the time that she once spent exclusively with you, and it's not unusual for partners to feel some jealousy in response to this new situation. I recall feeling confused and judgmental when faced with the reconfigured family situation. I wondered why my partner couldn't understand that my kids needed my time. After all, she was an adult who could take care of herself, but the children needed me –it was my job to take care of them. I eventually realized that even if my partner knew this on some level, it was still a loss and and very stressful to realize that she was receiving less from me than she had been getting and than she had expected to receive when we finally became a couple.

Perhaps the most common complaint I hear from couples who are creating a new lesbian family concerns the new partner's expectations of the children. She often feels that the mom is not consistent or strict enough when the kids are being difficult. I am assuming your partner is coming into your family without any children of her own. The parent who has lived with her children since they were born usually has learned to ignore many annoying kid behaviors and to pick and choose her battles. Your partner doesn't have that experience. Her tolerance is probably lower than yours for that reason. If your partner is like mine was, she probably wants you to set more rules and assign consequences to misbehavior. These are areas that have to be discussed with empathy and sensitivity on both parts in order to find new parenting patterns that meet somewhere in the middle.

Having worked therapeutically with many stepfamily couples, I have found that lesbians who have never parented are often worried about being accepted by their partner's children. They may also feel insecure about being a good parental figure. Their role can be confusing. As a parent, you may need to clarify how you want your partner to be involved in the parenting. If you want her advice, it's generally best given when the two of you are alone. If you ask your partner to discipline your kids, you may be setting her up for negative reactions from your kids. She will have a better relationship with the children if you take the disciplinarian role when necessary and allow your partner to develop a friendly adult role, while supporting your authority.

It's important to talk directly with your partner about these issues and, if necessary, find a couples' therapist to help you to address them as early as possible. Sometimes there is no clear resolution to the conflicting needs of you, your partner, and your children. However, feeling understood by your partner is often enough to get you through the difficult adjustment. It can be challenging to just listen and empathize with each other's desires and complaints, but learning to do so will set the groundwork for a satisfying long-term relationship.

REFERENCES

Blumenfeld, Warren & Raymond, Diane. *Looking at Gay and Lesbian Life*. Boston: Beacon Press, 1993.

Burns, David, M.D. (1990) *The Feeling Good Handbook*. Plume, 1990.

Chodron, Pema. *When Things Fall Apart: Heart Advice for Difficult Times*. Boston: Shambhala, 2000.

Corvino, John, ed. *Same Sex: Debating the Ethics, Science, and Culture of Homosexuality*. New York: Rowman & Littlefield, 1997.

Diamond, Lisa M. *Sexual Fluidity: Understanding Women's Love and Desire*. Cambridge: Harvard University Press, 2008.

Esterberg, Kristin G., ed. *Lesbian and Bisexual Identities*. Philadelphia: Temple University Press, 1997.

Kasl, Charlotte, Ph.D. *If the Buddha Dated*. New York: Penguin Books, 1999.

Lessor, Elizabeth. *Broken Open: How Difficult Times Can Help Us Grow*. New York: Villard, 2005.

Klein, Fritz & Wolf, Timothy, eds. *Two Lives to Lead: Bisexuality in Men and Women*. New York: Harrington Park Press, 1985.

Prather, Hugh. *Notes on Love and Courage*. Canari Press, 2001

Remen, Rachel Naomi, M.D. *Kitchen Table Wisdom*. New York: Penguin Group, 1996.

Wallerstein, Judith S., and Bakerslee, Sandra. *What About the Kids?: Raising Your Children Before, During and After the Divorce*. New York: Hyperion, 2003.

RESOURCES

Books

Abbott, Deborah & Farmer, Ellen, Editors. *From Wedded Wife to Lesbian Life*. California: The Crossing Press, 1995.

Atkins, Dawn, ed. *Bisexual Women in the Twenty-First Century*. New York: Harrington Park Press, 2002.

Buxton, Amity Pierce. *The Other Side of the Closet: The Coming-Out Crisisfor Straight Spouses and Families*. New York: John Wiley & Sons, 1994.

Buxton, Amity Pierce. "From Hostile to Helpful," in Jess Wells, ed., *Home Fronts*. Alyson Press, 2000.

Cassingham, Barbee & O'Neil, Sally. *And Then I Met This Woman: Previously Married Women's Journeys into Lesbian Relationships*. Soaring Eagle Publishers, 2002.

Eichberg, Rob. *Coming Out: An Act of Love*. New York: Penguin Books, 1990.

Fisher, Bruce and Alberti, Robert. *Rebuilding: When Your Relationship Ends*. California: Impact Publishers, 2000.

Garner, Abigail. *Families Like Mine: Children of Gay Parents Tell It Like It Is*. New York: Harper Collins, 2004.

Jensen, Karol L. *Lesbian Epiphanies: Women Coming Out Later in Life*. New York: Harrington Park Press, 1999.

Lesser, Elizabeth. *Broken Open: How Difficult Times Can Help Us Grow.* New York: Villard, 2004.

Loulan, JoAnn. *Lesbian Sex.* San Francisco: Spinsters Ink, 1984.

Sachs, Rhona. *The Art of Meeting Women: A Guide for Gay Women.* New York: Slope Books, 1998.

Sauerman, Tom. "Coming Out to Your Parents." PFLAG (Parents, Families & Friends of Lesbians and Gays) pamphlet.

Signorile, Michelangelo. *Outing Yourself.* New York: Random House, 1995.

Strock, Carren. *Married Women Who Love Women.* New York: Doubleday, 1998.

Walsh, Candace & Andre, Laura. *Dear John, I Love Jane.* Berkeley, California: Seal Press, 2010.

Some Titles Suggested by the "Ask Joanne" Online Community

Blitzer, Lauren Levin. *Same Sex in the City: So Your Prince Charming Is Really a Cinderella.* New York: Simon and Schuster, 2006.

Corwin, Glenda. *Sexual Intimacy for Women.* Berkeley, California: Seal Press, 2010.

Kirshenbaum, Mira: *When Good People Have Affairs.* New York: St. Martin's Press, 2008.

Newman, Felice. *The Whole Lesbian Sex Book.* California: Cleis Press, 2004.

McCoy, Robin. *Late Bloomers: Awakening to Lesbianism After Forty.* Nebraska: Writers Club Press, 2000.

Books for Children

Abramchik, Lois. *Is Your Family Like Mine?* Brooklyn, NY: Open Heart, Open Mind Publishing, 1993. (Ages 4-8)

Edmunds, Barbara Lynn. *When Grown-Ups Fall in Love.* Eugene, OR: Hundreth Munchy Publications, 2000.

Newman, Leslea. *Heather Has Two Moms.* Google Books Twentieth Anniversary Edition, 2012.

Online resource: Gay, Lesbian, & Straight Education Network (GLSEN): *Annotated Bibliography of Children's Books with Gay & Lesbian Characters.* Resources for   Early Childhood Educators.

Classic Fiction with Lesbian Characters or Themes

Brown, Rita Mae. *Rubyfruit Jungle.* NY: Bantam Books, 1980.

Forrest, Katherine. *Curious Wine.* Kansas City, MO: Naiad Press, 1983.

Waters, Sarah: *Tipping the Velvet.* New York, NY: Penguin Books, 1998.

Winterson, Jeanette: *Oranges Are Not the Only Fruit.* London: Pandora Press, 1985.

Current Award-Winning Lesbian Literature

Search online for award-winning fiction and non-fiction on the website for Lambda Literary Award winners. *Lambdaliterary.org/awards.*

Note about Internet Searches and Virtual Communities

The internet and social networking has made it much easier to find supportive and safe communities. Try search terms like "married women coming out" and "married woman in love with a woman" on the main search engines like Google and Yahoo. Look for supportive virtual communities on social networking sites like Facebook, Twitter, and LinkedIn, all of which could provide resources and connections to women who are experiencing the same issues you are; in addition, these sites can link you to others with whom you might develop face to face relationships. Try doing simple searches for like-minded groups, using phrases like "older women coming out," "married women coming out," or "married women in love with women" on sites like Meetup, Craigslist, Facebook, Twitter, and Google Plus. Once you become comfortable getting together with other people, Meetup has groups and gatherings located everywhere. Try doing a search in your area for lesbian support groups. Even Goodreads, a social networking site where members can share comments and discussion about books they are reading, might be a good place to find a virtual community of women who are reading about and thinking about the same issues you are.

Internet Sites

About.com-Lesbian Life. *lesbianlife.about.com*. Wonderfully informative and comprehensive site that includes the Five Best Dating Sites for Lesbians, issues regarding coming out, diversity, home & family, sex, love, and relationships, and dating tips.

Lavender Visions. *lavendervisions.com*. Joanne Fleisher's website offers online support as well as advice for married lesbians, e-mail lists for women coming out later in life, and helpful resources. Describes services, including therapy, phone consultation & workshops for married women.

Divorce Support. *divorcesupport.com*. Provides resources relating to divorce.

Divorce Net. *divorcenet.com*. Family law advice.

Ivillage. *ivillage.com.* Offers advice about divorce and money. It has many articles on child custody and your rights in the divorce process.

Gay Law Net. *gaylawnet.com.* A national compilation of gay-friendly attorneys, with information about laws affecting the gay community in your state.

Living Fabulous. *livingfabulous.org/mor.* "The Mixed Orientation Marriage section of Living Fabulous is designed specifically to offer information and support to bisexuals who are married to a heterosexual and to provide helpful information to their heterosexual partners." (members-only site).

Making Mixed-Orientation Marriages Work. *http://groups.yahoo. com/group/MMOMW.*

A members-only online support group for both straight spouses of LGBT-questioning individuals and the married LGBT-questioning individuals themselves.

Straight Spouse Network. *straightspouse.org/home.php.* A support network for heterosexual spouses and partners of gay, lesbian, bisexual, and transgendered mates. Provides support and resources.

Family Support Sites

COLAGE: Children of Lesbians and Gays Everywhere. *colage. org.* Provides support services for children of LGBT parents.

Families Like Mine. *familieslikemine.com.* Information for people from families with gay or lesbian parents. Based on Abigail Garner's book with the same title.

Family Pride Coalition. *familypride.org.* Information about gay, lesbian, bisexual, and transgendered parents and parenting, as well as sexual orientation concerns. Lists local support groups across the country.

Human Rights Campaign (HRC) Family Project. *hrc.org/issues/parenting.* HRC provides current resources that address the many potential paths to parenthood, as well as issues around LGBT youth and families in schools.

Lesbian Mom Today. *lesbianmomtoday.com.* An active website full of articles on lesbian parenting and many other issues.

Mombian. *Mombian.com.* A blog offering a mix of parenting, politics, diversions and resources for lesbian moms.

PFLAG (Parents and Friends of Lesbians and Gays. *community.pflag.org.* Support for husbands and families. Meetings at many locations across the country.

Gay-Friendly Religious Organizations & Resources

Coming Out Christian. *cmgoutchristian.wordpress.com.* A blog focusing on building bridges and promoting love and understanding between the Church and the LGBT community.

Dignity. *dignityusa.org.* LGBT Catholics working for justice and respect for all persons in the Catholic church. Local Chapters worship across the U.S.

Evangelical Network. *t-e-n.org.* An association of LGBT-affirming evangelical ministries and individuals.

Integrity. *integrityusa.org.* LGBT Episcopalian organization across the U.S. offering worship, education, outreach, and service to the church.

Metropolitan Community Church. *mcchurch.org.* A LGBT Christian church, proclaiming inclusivity and community, social action, and justice with churches across the U.S.

Keshet. *keshetonline.org*. A national grassroots organization that works for the full inclusion of gay, lesbian, bisexual, and transgender (GLBT) Jews in Jewish life.

Sister Friends Together. *sisterfriends-together.org*. Online Christian faith community providing practical resources and a forum for spiritual reflections relevant to the lives of Christian lesbian, bisexual and transgender women.

Unitarian Universalist Church. *uua.org*. Gay-welcoming church that includes wisdom from the world's teachings, including Jewish, Christian, Humanist, and spiritual traditions.

World Congress of GLBT Jewish Organizations. *glbtjews.org*. Holds conferences and workshops representing the interests of GLBT Jews around the world.

Made in the USA
Middletown, DE
23 November 2015